# J. G. FARRELL

## RONALD BINNS

METHUEN
LONDON AND NEW YORK

*For my brother, James Binns*

*First published in 1986 by*
*Methuen & Co. Ltd*
*11 New Fetter Lane, London EC4P 4EE*
*Published in the USA by*
*Methuen & Co.*
*in association with Methuen, Inc.*
*29 West 35th Street, New York, NY 10001*

© *1986 Ronald Binns*

*Typeset by Rowland Phototypesetting Ltd*
*Printed in Great Britain by*
*Richard Clay (The Chaucer Press) Ltd*
*Bungay, Suffolk*

*British Library Cataloguing in Publication Data*

Binns, Ronald
J. G. Farrell. – (Contemporary writers)
1. Farrell, J. G. – Criticism and interpretation
I. Title   II. Series
823'.914     PR6056.A75Z

ISBN 0-416-40320-4

*Library of Congress Cataloging in Publication Data*
Binns, Ronald, 1948–
J. G. Farrell.

(Contemporary writers)
Bibliography: p.
1. Farrell, J. G. (James Gordon), 1935–
Criticism and interpretation.
I. Title.   II. Series.
PR6056.A75Z57   1986
823'.914     86-695

ISBN 0-416-40320-4 (pbk.)

# CONTENTS

# GENERAL EDITORS' PREFACE

The contemporary is a country which we all inhabit, but there is little agreement as to its boundaries or its shape. The serious writer is one of its most sensitive interpreters, but criticism is notoriously cautious in offering a response or making a judgement. Accordingly, this continuing series is an endeavour to look at some of the most important writers of our time, and the questions raised by their work. It is, in effect, an attempt to map the contemporary, to describe its aesthetic and moral topography.

The series came into existence out of two convictions. One was that, despite all the modern pressures on the writer and on literary culture, we live in a major creative time, as vigorous and alive in its distinctive way as any that went before. The other was that, though criticism itself tends to grow more theoretical and apparently indifferent to contemporary creation, there are grounds for a lively aesthetic debate. This series, which includes books written from various standpoints, is meant to provide a forum for that debate. By design, some of those who have contributed are themselves writers, willing to respond to their contemporaries; others are critics who have brought to the discussion of current writing the spirit of contemporary criticism or simply a conviction, forcibly and coherently argued, for the contemporary significance of their subjects. Our aim, as the series develops, is to continue to explore the works of major post-war writers – in fiction, drama and poetry – over an international range, and thereby to illuminate not only those works but also in some degree the artistic, social and moral assumptions on which they rest. Our wish is that, in their very variety of approach and emphasis, these books will stimulate interest in and understanding of the vitality of a living literature which, because it is contemporary, is especially ours.

*Norwich, England*

MALCOLM BRADBURY
CHRISTOPHER BIGSBY

# PREFACE AND ACKNOWLEDGEMENTS

When in 1973 *The Siege of Krishnapur* won the Booker Prize, Britain's most prestigious annual literary award, it brought J. G. Farrell to public attention for the first time in his writing career. Farrell was 38 and *The Siege of Krishnapur* was his fifth novel. This novel, set against the background of the Indian Mutiny, was the second volume in a trilogy about the decline of the British Empire which was probably the most ambitious literary project conceived and executed by any British novelist in the 1970s. The prize served to direct attention to the earlier, neglected volume *Troubles* (1970), a haunting, whimsical and poetic novel now often identified as Farrell's masterpiece. The third and final volume, *The Singapore Grip*, Farrell's longest, most cerebral and ambitious work, appeared five years after the Booker award, in 1978, shortly before his tragically early death at the age of 44.

Farrell, born in 1935, has since been hailed as one of the finest novelists of his generation. Praise for his work has come from writers as diverse as Elizabeth Bowen, Francis King, A. N. Wilson, Paul Theroux and Margaret Drabble. Farrell's fiction has now begun to exert its influence upon other contemporary writers; William Boyd's *An Ice-Cream War* (1982) owes much to Farrell's absurdist view of war and imperial folly, while *Troubles* stands behind the Welsh writer Mary Jones's *Resistance* (1985), a novel about nationalism and sickness set in a rambling hotel.

Farrell's novels are compellingly readable and his belief in the importance of a strong narrative drive and a solidly established plot and characterization has won his books a wide audience. His fiction contains elements of popular narrative modes – the fairy story, the adventure story, the 'blockbuster' – but Farrell treats them ironically and his novels convey a distinctively dark, idiosyncratic, tragicomic picture of existence. Farrell's early novels cannot be ignored in any assessment of his career, for it is in works like *The Lung* (1965) and *A Girl in the Head* (1967) that his vision of a grotesque and discomforting comic universe first appears. The major focus of an examination of Farrell's *oeuvre* must inevitably be the Empire novels, with their unifying theme of the collapse of apparently stable and ordered societies under the pressure of internal contradictions and destructive forces which impinge from outside. Although Farrell's was a strikingly original talent his career did not develop in a vacuum, and part of the purpose of this study is to show how it was that a novelist from an Anglo-Irish background whose sensibility has often been described as 'bizarre' and 'eccentric' was attracted to the genre of the historical novel and what uses he made of this relatively unpopular form.

I would like to thank J. G. Farrell's family for their kindness in assisting me with biographical enquiries. In particular I owe a special debt to his mother, Jo Farrell. I am also very grateful to Dr Bridget O'Toole and Helen Dady for their help and to the Phoenix Trust, administered by the Society of Authors, for its generosity in providing a research award towards the writing of this book.

The author and publisher would like to thank the following for permission to quote copyright material: Century Hutchinson for extracts from *A Man From Elsewhere* and *The Lung*; Jonathan Cape and Fontana for extracts from *A Girl in the Head* and *Troubles*; Weidenfeld & Nicolson and Fontana for extracts from *The Siege of Krishnapur*, *The Singapore Grip* and *The Hill Station*; and the Estate of the late J. G. Farrell.

*London, England, 1985*                    RONALD BINNS

# A NOTE ON THE TEXTS

Page references for quotations from J. G. Farrell's writings are taken from the editions listed below. The following abbreviations have been used:

## Works by J. G. Farrell

MFE    *A Man From Elsewhere* (London: Hutchinson, 1963)
L    *The Lung* (London: Hutchinson, 1965)
GIH    *A Girl in the Head* (London: Fontana, 1981)
T    *Troubles* (London: Flamingo, 1984)
SK    *The Siege of Krishnapur* (London: Flamingo, 1985)
SG    *The Singapore Grip* (London: Flamingo, 1984)
HS    *The Hill Station, an unfinished novel.* With Two Appreciations and a Personal Memoir, and an Indian Diary (London: Fontana, 1982)
P    'The Pussycat Who Fell in Love with the Suitcase', *Atlantis* (Winter 1973/74), pp. 6–10.
B    Untitled essay in *Bookmarks*, ed. Frederick Raphael (London: Quartet, 1975), pp. 49–52.

## Interviews

MD1    Malcolm Dean, 'An Insight Job', *Guardian*, 1 September 1973.
CM    Caroline Moorehead, 'Writing in the dark, and not a detail missed', *The Times*, 9 September 1978.
MD2    Malcolm Dean, 'Grip of Empire', *Guardian*, 13 September 1978.
GB    George Brock, 'Epitaph for the Empire', *Observer Magazine*, 24 September 1978, pp. 73, 75.

11

# 1

## STATES OF SIEGE

His notebooks comprise a sort of chronicle of those strange
early days we all lived through. But an unusual type of
chronicle, since the writer seems to make a point of under-
statement, and at first sight we might almost imagine that
[he] had a habit of observing events and people through the
wrong end of a telescope. In those chaotic times he set
himself to recording the history of what the normal historian
passes over. (Albert Camus, *The Plague*)

In 1974 J. G. Farrell wrote:

There are, it is agreed, a hundred thousand ways of writing a
novel and an equal variety of intentions that may be given
substance in a novel. A reader may pick and choose among
this variety as great a number as he wants, but ordinarily a
writer must choose only one way to write. This being so, I
believe (subject to all possible later changes of mind) that the
qualities of Conrad and Hughes are those which accord most
closely to my own conception of what goes to make a good
novel. (*B*)

The qualities which Farrell particularly admired in the fiction
of Joseph Conrad and Richard Hughes were 'the relaxed tone,
the hallucinating clarity of image, and the concreteness that
gives substance to [their] vision', and they are qualities which
Farrell's best writing shares.

In addition, although Conrad and Hughes had a keen sense
of plot and began by writing fiction partly rooted in the
conventions of the adventure story, both were later drawn, as
Farrell was, to major historical themes. *Nostromo* (1904) is one
of the classic novels of imperialism; *Under Western Eyes* (1911)
is centred around the activities of Russian revolutionaries,

and when he died Conrad was working on a novel about Napoleon. Hughes's *The Fox in the Attic* (1961) and *The Wooden Shepherdess* (1973) both focused on the rise of the Nazis between 1923 and 1934 and were intended to form the first two volumes of a massive historical epic entitled 'The Human Predicament' (subsequently left incomplete at the time of Hughes's death in 1976). Elsewhere, Farrell wrote

> there is no more difficult feat than to portray a historical person in fiction. Among English novels I can only think of one in which this has been done convincingly: the portrait of Hitler in Richard Hughes's *The Fox in the Attic*.[1]

In Farrell's case his importance as a novelist rests entirely on his three historical novels: *Troubles* (1970), set against the background of the Irish disturbances of 1919–21; *The Siege of Krishnapur* (1973), about a fictional episode in the 1857 Indian Mutiny; and *The Singapore Grip* (1978), a semi-documentary narrative about the period leading up to the surrender of Singapore to the Japanese during the Second World War.

The historical novel is not a genre which has held much appeal for British novelists. It is traditionally regarded as having originated with *Waverley* (1814) and other novels by Sir Walter Scott, but Scott's influence in Britain seems to have been much greater upon the popular historical romance than on the serious novel. The nature of British society and culture over the past two hundred years seems to provide a substantial reason for this lack of interest in the genre by this country's novelists. In his classic study *The Historical Novel* (1937), Georg Lukács argued that the sudden flowering of the European historical novel was associated with the French Revolution, the revolutionary wars and the rise and fall of Napoleon, sweeping events 'which for the first time made history a *mass experience*, and moreover on a European scale'.[2] Britain was the great exception. In neither the nineteenth nor twentieth centuries has Britain experienced foreign invasion, occupation, military dictatorship or the violent overthrow of monarchy or government. Thus when the great Victorian novelists tried their hand at historical novels they were not writing out of any kind of personal experience of historical upheaval. George Eliot's *Romola* (1862–3) is, notoriously, a lifeless exercise in historical reconstruction. Similarly *A Tale of Two Cities* (1859) says rather more about Dickens's own anxieties than it does about French history (in *The Singapore Grip* the Frenchman Dupigny complains that when the British think of France 'it is always in the manner of that *grand emmerdeur*, Charles Dickens' (*SG*, p. 124)). Finally, Thackeray's *The History of Henry Esmond* (1852) is likely to be limited for many modern readers by its benign soft-focus view of history as an amiable comedy. In the century of napalm, Auschwitz and the Gulag archipelago we live, in George Steiner's sombre phrase, in a post-culture.

But even in the twentieth century no significant, innovative historical novel tradition has developed in Britain. The experience of world war resulted in a variety of autobiographical novels with an historical setting, ranging from Frederick Manning's *The Middle Parts of Fortune* (1929) to Olivia Manning's Balkan and Levant trilogies, but these novels have generally been written within the conventions of an orthodox, stylistically conservative realism.

J. G. Farrell's Empire trilogy provides a striking exception to this often rather unadventurous type of writing. During the 1960s Farrell came to regard contemporary British fiction as narrow, conventional and impoverished in its subject matter and stylistic resource. *The Singapore Grip* contains a satirical reference to a young man who eccentrically keeps in his refrigerator

the manuscript of a novel he was writing about a gifted young American from Kansas City who goes to Oxford on a scholarship and there, having fallen in love with an English girl who surrounds herself with cynical, sophisticated people, goes to the dogs, forgetting the sincere, warm-hearted American girl whose virginity he had made away with while crossing the Atlantic on a Cunard liner. (*SG*, p. 283)

Farrell makes clear his scorn for a certain sort of provincial social novel which traditionally has enjoyed great success in Britain (the contents of a refrigerator, we may recall, are usually frozen or preserved and decidedly inert). Farrell's joke is partly at his own expense, since he came to regard his own early fiction as callow and unsatisfactory. He himself abandoned a semi-autobiographical novel about an Englishman in New York and, while living in that city, began writing *Troubles*, his first historical novel. The hero of this abandoned novel is a biologist specializing in the effects of freezing and supercooling, the symbolic thrust of which is underlined by his complaint to a close woman friend that she merely wishes to keep him in a refrigerator until she can make emotional use of him. Ironically the young man in *The Singapore Grip* recognizes that his novel is 'rubbish' but cannot quite bring himself to destroy the manuscript, musing that perhaps he will be able to convert it 'into an epic of Tolstoyan dimensions' (*SG*, pp. 283–4). Later, when he had completed his Empire trilogy, Farrell explained what had led him in the 1960s to abandon fiction set in the present and turn instead to the past for his narrative material:

> People's minds are made up about what is happening now. I used to read novel scripts for Hutchinson's, the publishers. In the mid-1960s they were all writing about Aldermaston, and for all I know they still are. It seemed to me that none of these novels really worked. They were involved with emotions that were satiated, about which people had fixed views. What I most wanted to do was create a new world into which I could bring what I wanted and control the reactions of the reader. I want to hypnotise the reader. (GB)

Farrell's chosen theme, the decline of the British Empire, was an ambitious one. In the same interview he remarked, 'It seemed to me that the really interesting thing that's happened during my lifetime has been the decline of the British Empire. When I was a child it was very much a going concern.' In 1918 the Empire contained over a quarter of the world's population and dominated over a quarter of the world's land surface. Fifty years later virtually all British colonies had been granted independence and Britain had become in essence a solely European power: 'So far as the end of the British Empire can be set at a definite point of time, it was the afternoon of 19 January 1968, when the Labour Prime Minister, Harold Wilson, announced the final homecoming of the British legions.'[3] Farrell's trilogy is implicitly about the decline of modern Britain and significantly he selected moments in history which involved blows to imperial self-esteem and a loss of cultural self-confidence.

Farrell's life and family background provide some significant pointers to the sources of his creative inspiration and to the eclectic, original way in which he came to treat the subject of imperial entropy. James Gordon Farrell was born on 23 January 1935 in a nursing home at 150 Moscow Drive, Liverpool, not far from where his parents lived at 15 Hampton Court Road. His mother, Prudence Josephine Farrell (née Russell) had been born and brought up in Ireland, the daughter of an English timber dealer. In 1930 she married William Francis Farrell, the son of a Liverpool wine merchant. J. G. Farrell's birth certificate lists his father's occupation as a produce broker's clerk, but subsequently he spent many years abroad working as an accountant. Mr and Mrs Farrell's first child, Robert, was born in 1932; a third son, Richard, was born in 1943. Even as a young child J. G. Farrell wrote little stories and apparently he had a keen sense of observation. He was an early reader: the first book Farrell read was Scott's *Ivanhoe*, which, he shrewdly told his mother, had a wonderful story spoiled by long boring descriptions of scenery.

When war broke out in 1939 the Farrell family moved to 'Boscobel', an enormous rambling Victorian house in Southport which Mrs Farrell had inherited from an uncle. The house had numerous bedrooms and soon filled up with homeless relatives and friends. The tranquillity of life in Southport was rudely shattered in the spring of 1941 when a German bomber heading for the Liverpool docks was attacked by a fighter plane and jettisoned a stick of bombs overhead. The blast hit 'Boscobel', ripping off part of the roof and blowing in the doors and windows; the house next door was flattened and its occupants killed. Miraculously, despite all the broken glass and flying masonry, no one in 'Boscobel' was seriously injured. The young Jim Farrell was subsequently quoted on the incident by the *Southport Gazette*. 'This man Hitler', he stoutly told a reporter, 'really is a nuisance' (he was not to be interviewed again by a journalist until thirty-two years later, when *The Siege of Krishnapur* was published). Farrell was 6 years old at the time of this bomb attack on his home, and from the evidence of his mature fiction it seems to have made an immense impression upon him. Years later when, as a successful novelist, he had started to give interviews, Farrell alluded to the way in which his experiences as a child during the blitz had influenced his fictional treatment of possessions: 'I remember ... how adults in pyjamas would assemble in our air-raid shelter clutching the most extraordinary objects. During the Indian mutiny, Cawnpore was made almost indefensible by pianos and stuffed owls and other bric-à-brac' (MD2). He also explained that the theme of a besieged community held metaphysical overtones. A siege, he remarked, 'is a microcosm of real life and [the] human condition – *hostility all around you with the individual in a rather temporary shelter*' (MD1, my italics). It was around this time that Farrell wrote his first short story, which began 'Bang, bang, bang, the Indians are coming' – ironically a kind of rudimentary blueprint for the Empire novels, each of which deals with the theme of an embattled community threatened by alien forces.

The 1941 bombing episode sheds an interesting light on the development of Farrell's Empire trilogy. In *Troubles* the scene is an enormous rambling Victorian hotel, a vast, crumbling structure with innumerable rooms, dark corridors and forgotten wings. It is inhabited by an eccentric collection of Anglo-

Irish guests and under threat from incomprehensible and violent outsiders. A number of commentators have noted how similar the materials of *Troubles* are to Farrell's previous novel *A Girl in the Head* (1967), which also features a gallery of eccentrics living in a rambling household beside the sea – a household identified in a scene in which the novel's prematurely old hero scans the landscape through binoculars and sees 'a couple of other houses and (so close that it appeared merely as a mist of pink brick) the Victorian mansion called Boscobel in which he himself lived' (*GIH*, p. 11). *Troubles* begins with an image of desolation and ruin – 'the charred remains of the enormous main building' (*T*, p. 10) – before tracking back in time to show how this enchanted dream-like world came to be destroyed. The theme of refugees crowded into a building which is under threat recurs in *The Siege of Krishnapur*, in which a collection of middle-class Victorians in a remote Indian town retreat into the Residency and are then besieged by mutinous sepoys firing rockets. The physical destruction of a familiar and loved room makes an unforgettable impression upon 'the Collector', the Residency's chief occupant:

> his shattered bedroom slowly materialized out of the darkness, the splintered woodwork, the broken furniture, the wallpaper hanging in shreds from the shrapnel-pocked walls; this once beautiful, complacent, happy, elegant room was like a physical manifestation of his own grieving mind (*SK*, p. 226).

Shortly afterwards, staring through a telescope, he witnesses a huge explosion that bursts

> with a flash that burnt itself so deeply into the Collector's brain that he reeled. . . . And then there was nothing but smoke, dust, debris, and a crash which dropped a picture from the wall behind him. But at the next instant from the other side of the Residency echoed another, even greater explosion . . . and that was the last of Dr Dunstaple's house (*SK*, 237–8).

Both 'Kilnalough', the setting of *Troubles*, and 'Krishnapur' are fictional places, whereas the setting of Farrell's third Empire novel, Singapore, is of course real. In *The Singapore Grip* the mood shifts from the enclosed, mythic, dreamlike half-real worlds of the two earlier historical novels to a harsh, sprawling modern setting. *The Singapore Grip* contains many realistic scenes of buildings and people being attacked from the air and, fascinatingly, is set largely in 1941, the very year of the bomb attack on the Farrell household. Indeed, there is even what sounds very much like a fictionalization of the 'Boscobel' bombing episode in Farrell's account of what happened to the Langfield family:

> The Langfields had suffered a misfortune. A bomb jettisoned at random by a Japanese plane had fallen in Nassim Road, partly destroying the house. None of them had been hurt, except for a few scratches. (*SG*, p. 400)

Once again the surprise of being bombed makes a profound impression on the chief occupant, Mr Langfield, who 'had reached the age when a person finds it hard to adjust to a sudden shock like the destruction of his house' (*SG*, p. 401). The experience of being bombed at the age of 6 was the first of two shocks in Farrell's life profoundly to affect his creative vision of the world. The second one, however, did not occur until some fifteen years later.

In 1945 the Farrell family moved to Ireland and went to live in Saval Park Road, Dalkey (where the young J. G. Farrell later made an anagram out of his address and submitted a number of unsuccessful tongue-in-cheek sentimental love stories to publishers under the pseudonym 'Dora Park-Saval'). Between the ages of 12 and 18 Farrell, like his two brothers, was sent as a boarder to Rossall School, Fleetwood, on the Lancashire coast (the hero of *The Lung* (1965) recalls his time as 'A lonely schoolboy, cloistered in a boarding school throughout his adolescence' (*L*, p. 46)). Farrell claimed that in Ireland he was always regarded as English but that in England he was always treated as if he was Irish. Rossall School had its positive side, however, for it was here that he encountered Pierre Loti's *Pêcheur d'Islande* (1886), which Farrell later described as 'the trap door through which, without in the least intending to, I would crawl into another culture' (*B*). Loti (1850–1923) is little known in Britain although he was greatly admired by Proust, and Edmund Gosse once identified his exotic travel novels as 'long sobs of remorseful memory' (*B*); John Carey has described Loti's prose as 'voluptuous, dream-like (and untranslatable)'.[4] Farrell found himself entranced by *Pêcheur d'Islande*: 'So powerful an impression did this book make on me that today there are certain phenomena for which an expression of Loti's will alone suffice. A certain wintry light over the sea, for example, still conjures up Loti's "*lumière blafarde*"' (*B*). Farrell eagerly devoured other novels by Loti, finding them manifestly unlike anything he had ever read in English. They prepared him for an adolescent devotion to Colette and, later, Stendhal. If Loti and Colette led him to the dreamlike, hallucinatory prose of Hughes and Conrad, Stendhal helped Farrell towards Tolstoy and an absurdist view of history and warfare:

> My view of the way things happen contains an awful lot of things historians never consider, because I can introduce things that are much too trivial. The real experience is not composed of treaties being signed or pincer movements. It's smoke in your eyes or having a blister on your foot. It's funny the way certain novelists have taken over certain historical events as the dominant description which stays in people's minds: Tolstoy's account of Napoleon's Russian campaign or Stendhal's character at Waterloo. (GB)

After leaving Rossall School Farrell taught for a year in a Dublin prep school. Farrell, it seems, was not greatly impressed by Dublin, regarding it as provincial and claustrophobic. Martin Sands, the gaunt hero of *The Lung*, permits himself a few scornful Joycean reflections about his Dublin past: 'What in hell would Martin Sands, the demi-skeleton, find to do in a place like that? . . . Dublin is the friendliest and most insensitive city in the world' (L, pp. 165–6). Farrell fled from Dublin and went to Canada 'to collect experience with which to become a "writer"', in part 'Propelled by dreams of Hemingway' (GB). In *The Lung* Sands recalls his 'brief, demonstrative, and utterly futile self-exile in Canada' (L, p. 55). Farrell lived on Baffin Island in the Canadian Arctic for seven months, working as labourer, fireman and then clerk on the military Defence Early Warning line. Afterwards Farrell toured Canada and the United States before returning home to Ireland.

In the autumn of 1956 Farrell went up to Brasenose College, Oxford, to read Law. Near the end of his first term Farrell was changing after a college rugby match when suddenly he collapsed. He woke up in hospital to discover that he had polio. Prior to the polio attack Farrell had been a healthy 12-stone 21-year-old, keen on sport. He was now transformed, literally overnight, into an invalid. His hair turned white, his weight shrank to 7 stone 6 pounds and he lost the use of both arms. He spent six months in a device, nowadays obsolete, known as an iron lung, which was used to administer prolonged artificial respiration by means of mechanical pumps. This painful and terrifying experience was subsequently enshrined in vividly realistic detail in Farrell's second novel. In the months and years that followed, regular visits to clinics and hospitals gradually enabled Farrell to regain the use of one arm. Farrell never really recovered from this experience and ultimately it may have contributed to his death, since he was unable to swim.

The episode was a traumatic one and Farrell was prey to phases of deep depression for a long time afterwards. Regan, the novelist in Farrell's first published novel *A Man From Elsewhere* (1963), looks back on

a period . . . when time had seemed to stand still, when the future had seemed a towering mountainface and each new hour a breathless, painful step in its ascent. In constant danger of slipping back he had hauled himself into the future with numb and bleeding fingers. (*MFE*, p. 110)

The bomb attack on 'Boscobel' in 1941 and the 1956 polio attack seem to have combined to colour Farrell's vision of human existence as frail, insecure and temporary. In Farrell's mature fiction human beings and their communities are in perpetual states of siege, battered by circumstance both from without and within. Illness is a powerful underlying metaphor in Farrell's historical novels and there is never any shortage of outside agencies to continue from the outside the disintegration which has already begun from within. Farrell diagnoses colonial societies which are collapsing simultaneously from the centre and from the edges, and these symptoms of collapse are manifested in characters who are themselves often ill, diseased or dying. Significantly the wisest, most detached and clearseeing characters in Farrell's novels are usually (although not invariably) doctors. In his last completed novel there appears a hideously decrepit dog which is comically christened 'the Human Condition'. The Human Condition is, we learn, 'diminutive, elderly and frail' (*SG*, p. 267). Towards the end of the book one of the characters observes 'objectively' that the wretched creature is 'rotting internally' (p. 482). Ironically, the dog makes a desperate bid for freedom and succeeds in escaping from the general conflagration that encompasses the doomed city of Singapore. It sails, an unwanted guest, on one of the last boats to leave before the arrival of the victorious Japanese – but whether or not the Human Condition finally reaches a safe port is left ambiguously open.

Farrell returned to Brasenose College in autumn 1957, switching to Modern Languages, which it was thought would be less taxing than Law. Farrell's brush with the prospect of death from poliomyelitis seems to have clarified and sharpened his previously rather vague aspirations to be a writer. He set to work on a novel entitled *Lung*, which was submitted to a number of publishers but turned down. The manuscript of *Lung* seems not to have survived but probably it was a raw, indulgent slice of autobiography, as first novels by aspiring writers often are.

In 1960 Farrell graduated with a BA Honours degree in

French and Spanish, Third Class. He then found employment in France, where he worked as a language teacher from 1961 to 1963. During this period Farrell wrote another novel, *A Man From Elsewhere* (1963), which was accepted by Hutchinson and published under a New Writers scheme designed to encourage young unknown novelists. The book was dedicated to Farrell's mother and father. Farrell was in France at a turbulent moment in modern history and the novel registers contemporary anxieties about torture in Algeria, plastic bomb atrocities in France, the atom bomb and the Berlin crisis. *A Man From Elsewhere* showed Farrell attempting to write a detached, non-autobiographical narrative dealing with political and historical themes (the main character is a hardline Communist journalist and the plot revolves around his visit to a famous dying novelist with the aim of unearthing material suitable for a defamation campaign). The novel was generously reviewed by David Holloway:

> I believe that the Anglo-Irish author of *A Man From Elsewhere* will be someone about whom a great deal will be heard in the future. Of course there are faults in this first novel, but they are good faults: the author tries to cram too much into too little space; there are loose ends; not all the characters justify their inclusion. On the other hand Mr Farrell shows that not only can he handle ideas, he is a story-teller as well. Altogether this is a most distinguished debut.[5]

After leaving France Farrell spent the mid-sixties in London, living in a succession of seedy bedsitters in the Notting Hill area. He survived financially by teaching English to foreigners and by reading manuscripts for Hutchinson's (an unsolicited manuscript entitled *A Weekend with Claude* received Farrell's enthusiastic recommendation and an unknown young writer called Beryl Bainbridge was duly launched upon her career). In London Farrell quickly followed up his first book with two fluent but uneven comic novels, *The Lung* (1965) and *A Girl in the Head* (1967). *The Lung* presumably cannibalized the materials of his first rejected novel and gives a realistic but also at times wildly comic account of the experiences of a man in an iron lung. 'The writing is crisp and evenly tensioned,' wrote one reviewer, 'and the description of what it feels like inside a lung has a horrible authenticity. This is a human and entertaining novel, and confirms Mr Farrell as a man with something to say and a highly skilful way of saying it.'[6] Farrell dedicated this second novel to his Oxford contemporary, Russell McCormmach, subsequently author of the novel *Night Thoughts of a Classical Physicist* (1982).

Farrell's third book, *A Girl in the Head* (an early version of which was entitled *The Succubus*), gives an account of the comic misadventures of a gloomy emigré aristocrat in a garish seaside resort. It is the most stylish of Farrell's early novels and its slightly flippant tone and typographical trickery are reminiscent of B. S. Johnson's *Travelling People* (1963). *A Girl in the Head* received some poor, even hostile reviews and Farrell's developing confidence received a jolt which may in part have contributed to the sudden change of direction in his writing. Having flirted with avant-garde techniques Farrell later reacted violently against them, criticizing (in a thinly veiled attack on Beckett's *Comment C'est* and B. S. Johnson's boxed novel *The Unfortunates*) 'those rather uninteresting mechanical feats, like writing a novel all in one sentence or making it out of loose-leafed pages which can be read in any order' (MD1).

In 1966 Farrell was awarded a Harkness Fellowship and set off to spend two years in North America. It was while he was living in New York that he decided to write a novel set in a time that was over. He chose Ireland in 1919–21, the popular name for this period – that of 'the troubles' – supplying Farrell with his title. Perhaps living in New York gave Farrell the distance he needed in space and time from his subject matter. Elizabeth Bowen shrewdly noted that although Farrell had spent his childhood in Ireland it had not been 'particularly rewardingly or willingly': 'This bending of his imagination upon Ireland cannot be nostalgic compulsion, or "the return

25

of the native" — yet could there, all the same, be some undertow?'[7]

Bowen also marvelled at how vividly Farrell had captured 'the authentic smell' of those times when the author himself had no personal memory of it:

> *Troubles* necessitated the exploration of a time outside his experience and far from it. How was he to enter its psychic atmosphere, even its social one? He could not have selected a time that was more fraught — it was for that reason, clearly, that he selected it. He can have had little to go on but faded hearsay, and the wreathings and writhings, so peculiar to Ireland, of accumulated myth.[8]

In fact the time and setting which Farrell chose did hold a personal significance for him. His family had Anglo-Irish roots and his mother had been brought up in a large, isolated house in Maryborough (now Port Laoise), in the heart of rural Ireland. Her father was English and a Protestant, and was attacked in the local press as 'an imported Englishman'. Farrell actually gives him a fleeting appearance in *Troubles* in the Spring ball scene where Edward steps forward to greet 'the large and jovial figure of Bob Russell, the timber merchant from Maryborough' (*T*, p. 344). The neighbourhood where the Russells lived was a hotbed of IRA activity and bridges were regularly blown up. Mrs Farrell vividly remembers the impact which the 1916 Easter Rising made upon her, even though she was just a girl at the time and living far away from Dublin. Farrell quizzed his mother at great length while writing *Troubles*, anxious to get the details of rural Irish life accurate.

In 1969, while he was completing *Troubles*, *A Girl in the Head* was published as a Pan paperback. The cover featured a studio photograph of a beach scene with a young woman friend of Farrell's sitting cross-legged and clad in a bikini while Farrell himself crouched out of sight beneath the artificial shore with just his head showing through the sand. This bizarre set-up seems to have inspired the scene at the end of *Troubles* in which the hero is captured by the IRA, buried up to his neck in the sand and left to drown.

When Farrell began writing *Troubles* he believed himself to be writing about situations and controversies in Irish history which were long dead. Ironically, as he completed the novel a whole new era of 'troubles' began in Northern Ireland:

> I would go up to the British Museum newspaper library to read the *Irish Times* for 1920 and come back, buying an evening paper on the Tube. It was uncanny: exactly the same things were happening again, sometimes even in the same streets in Belfast. (GB)

The year 1968 in particular was one of troubles on a massive, international scale, with civil war in Nigeria, the May events in France, the Tet offensive in Vietnam, the Soviet invasion of Czechoslovakia and 'the siege of Chicago' in the United States. In *The Historical Novel* (a book Farrell greatly admired) Lukács defined an authentic historical novel as 'one which would rouse the present, *which contemporaries would experience as their own pre-history*' (my italics).[9] Two Irish reviewers agreed that *Troubles* was, in this respect, a *tour de force*. Bridget O'Toole remarked that 'taking into account the different historical setting, it is extraordinary how much seems relevant':

> Only the very old Irish family doctor has truly understood the situation, and before absenting himself entirely from the company of the Anglo-Irish, he observes among other things that if the British intend to keep their hold on Ireland, it will take 'a huge army' to do it! Perhaps the best representation of the failure of Protestant and Catholic to communicate is the beautifully funny, but disturbing scene in which Edward and Mr Noonan . . . go searching each other in vain down the Majestic's unending corridors.[10]

Elizabeth Bowen concluded her lengthy appreciation of the book with the observation that '*Troubles* is . . . not a "period piece"; it is yesterday reflected in today's consciousness. The ironies, the disparities, the dismay, the sense of unavailingness are contemporary.'[11]

A. N. Wilson has even gone so far as to assert that Farrell's novels 'throw more light on the Harold [Wilson] Years than they do on the history of the Empire'.[12] Certainly it seems no coincidence that the composition of Farrell's trilogy took place in a period acutely aware of itself as one of historical upheaval and crisis. Significantly one of the most academically influential British literary texts at the time Farrell was writing *Troubles* was Frank Kermode's *The Sense of an Ending* (1967), which interrogated the idea of apocalypse as it related to fictional structure. As Kermode conceded, 'The apocalyptic types – empire, decadence and renovation, progress and catastrophe – are fed by history and underlie our ways of making sense of the world from where we stand, in the middest.'[13]

The historical context in which Farrell's Empire trilogy was written seems inescapably relevant. In their book *Post-War Britain: A Political History* (1979) Alan Sked and Chris Cook argue that after 1964 the stable social system and political institutions of the United Kingdom began to disintegrate, and this was certainly how some observers saw it at the time. In 1968 Alasdair MacIntyre, noting that the unemployment figures had risen to over half a million, asserted that 'what we are seeing is a major change in the social scene, a change which might well be called "The Strange Death of Social Democratic England".'[14]

To Farrell, however, contemporary British *writing* seemed flat and provincial. In August 1970 he complained, 'If one turns from reading Solzhenitsyn to our own writers (as I did this week) one is immediately struck by the thought that, by comparison, we have simply nothing worth writing about.'[15] It was around this time that Farrell moved to a small ground-floor flat at 16 Egerton Gardens, London SW3, where he was to write the second and third volumes of his trilogy. The concept of a linked trilogy had not yet fully crystallized in his mind. At first he contemplated writing a novel set in Mexico in the

1860s, based on the tragedy of the Austrian Archduke Maximilian and his wife Carlota. Farrell made copious notes about the historical background, drawn from Mariano Cuevas's *The Religious History of Mexico*, then abandoned the project. Next, Farrell conceived of a kind of sequel to *Troubles*, set in India at the time of the great Mutiny of 1857 and originally entitled *Difficulties*. The location of Farrell's new home, almost next door to the Victoria and Albert Museum, was marvellously appropriate to the subject matter of his new novel since, as Donald Horne points out in his book *The Great Museum*, this area of South Kensington, with its museums, halls and educational buildings, represents 'the voice of nineteenth-century capitalism at its most enlightened, buoyant with optimism and reason and a belief in improvement. Education, science, art and technology would bring light. Free enterprise would bring abundance to the world and this abundance facilitate eternal progress.'[16] Under the gothic canopy of the Albert Memorial sits Victoria's Prince Consort in gilt bronze, holding in his hands the catalogue of the Great Exhibition of 1851 – a catalogue which forms an ironic touchstone against which the nightmare of mutiny is repeatedly measured in *The Siege of Krishnapur*.

In deciding to write a novel set in India Farrell was once again drawing partly on his family history for inspiration. Farrell's parents had been married in Burma in 1930 and then went to live in Chittagong, East Bengal, where Mr Farrell took on the position of Manager for the Pure Cane Molasses Company. In those days Chittagong was a small isolated port with a population of only eighty or so Europeans. This was the period of the 'freedom riots' and the situation was threatening for the white expatriate population. Farrell's father was himself shot and wounded (although not seriously) in a raid on the armoury at Chittagong. Farrell showed a keen interest in his father's Indian experiences and subsequently dedicated the finished novel to him.

Unlike his parents Farrell had never been to India and so, having completed his library researches into the Mutiny, he travelled out there for the first time in 1971. The 'Indian Diary' which he kept on that occasion has been posthumously published as an appendix to Farrell's last, unfinished novel *The Hill Station* (1981). There are striking parallels between Farrell's fiction and this diary, with its comic anecdotes of undignified personal discomfort, its eye for the grotesque and bizarre, and its sense of the diarist's perplexity, frustration and compassion as he moves through a strange, alien and sometimes horrifying land. Farrell was not an autobiographical novelist, yet his fiction cannot neatly be separated off from his life (indeed, Farrell himself teasingly linked the two, not least by incorporating the names of actual friends like Bridget O'Toole, Margaret Dobbs, Russell McCormmach and Ron Rose into his novels). Farrell deployed a languid, relaxed, intimate tone of narrative voice in his historical novels which amounts almost to a persona. In his last completed work, *The Singapore Grip* (1978), Farrell steps forward to announce his presence as 'the author of this book writing busily in a small red notebook' (*SG*, p. 500). Typically, his presence in Singapore involves a modest quantity of the physical discomfort to which his characters are invariably subjected: Farrell laconically presents himself 'scratching his knuckles where some lonely, last-remaining mosquito . . . ignoring his dignified appearance, has not hesitated to bite him as he scribbles' (Ibid.). One interviewer, noting that *The Singapore Grip*, like *The Siege of Krishnapur*, sets idealistic characters against cynical ones, asked 'which is the real Farrell?':

They both are. Now one gets the upper hand, now the other. But as the years go by I'm afraid the idealist inside me gets thinner while the cynic and libertine puts on weight (MD2).

But this was Farrell speaking in 1978. Five years earlier the novelist publicly revealed a rather more politically committed side to his personality. In November 1973, shortly after publication, *The Siege of Krishnapur* won that year's Booker Prize, in the face of stiff competition from Iris Murdoch and Beryl

30

Bainbridge. At the award ceremony Farrell surprised everyone by making a fierce verbal attack on the donors of the prize, the multinational firm Booker-McConnell, bitterly accusing them of exploiting and underpaying their black employees in the West Indies.

In fact Farrell's interest in politics had developed many years earlier when he was a student at Oxford. His mother remembers Farrell developing into a passionate socialist and coming home in the holidays to rail against his bourgeois background. Farrell's friend the journalist Malcolm Dean identified the novelist as 'a romantic socialist idealist' (MD2) and recalls how Farrell used to mock people who spoke disdainfully of 'seychellists' (*HS*, p. 200). Farrell's years in France seem to have reinforced these leanings to the left – *A Man From Elsewhere*, apart from having a politically committed protagonist, refers to such topics as the use of torture by French troops in Algeria. Perhaps significantly, when Farrell first attempted to define his approach to the historical novel he quoted Jean-Paul Sartre, explaining that he wanted 'to show people "undergoing" history'.[17]

In 1972, when he was completing *The Siege of Krishnapur*, Farrell read about the fall of Singapore and thought it would make 'a good project for an ambitious novelist' (CM). The anger which Farrell displayed in his Booker acceptance speech regarding social injustice seems in part to have motivated him to extend his two linked historical novels into a trilogy and to look at the British Empire from an economic viewpoint. In fact *The Siege of Krishnapur* touches briefly on colonial exploitation – Mr Simmons of the opium factory explains that the balls of opium 'would fetch about seventy-six shillings, while to the *ryot* and his family the Government paid a mere four shillings a pound' (*SK*, pp. 88–9) – but now Farrell turned his attention to an enormous, encyclopaedic investigation of the rubber industry in Malaya. The result was a massive, polemical epic intertwining the fortunes of colonial capitalism and the doomed city of Singapore. Farrell's friend the playwright and critic John Spurling has recalled how disputatious the novelist became at this time, something he attributed to Farrell's first-hand experience of the misery of the Third World:

> It was as if the fuse lit by the Indian visit took longer to reach its powder keg than the book [i.e. *The Siege of Krishnapur*] took to write. . . . while he was writing *The Singapore Grip* Jim became uncharacteristically argumentative and assertive on socio-political topics.[18]

Farrell returned to the Third World in 1975, spending part of his Booker money on two months in Singapore and the Far East, including a visit to the besieged city of Saigon (now Ho-Chi-Minh City) shortly before the final evacuation of US troops. The fall of Singapore appealed to Farrell as a subject because it was 'an episode of British history largely left alone by historians perhaps . . . because it was a defeat not a victory' (CM). Like Solzhenitsyn in *Lenin in Zurich* (1975), another historical novelist concerned to persuade us of the documentary veracity underlying his fiction, Farrell appended a bibliography to his novel.

When *The Singapore Grip* was published reviewers were more or less evenly divided between those who agreed with Margaret Drabble that it was classic Farrell – 'a fine piece of work, solid, informative, funny, tragic, one of those novels that present a whole world for the reader'[19] – and those who complained that Farrell had failed successfully to integrate his massively detailed researches into economics and war-time history with the story of his characters' lives. The young novelist Timothy Mo described the book as 'by far [Farrell's] most ambitious; happily, *The Singapore Grip* is also this brilliantly idiosyncratic and funny writer's most successful yet', adding that 'The novel may be Farrell's private attempt at *War and Peace*.'[20] The Irish writer Derek Mahon agreed that *The Singapore Grip* was Farrell's 'finest book', asserting that the three books in the trilogy were 'poems in prose as well as historical reconstructions and comic masterpieces'.[21]

With the trilogy completed Farrell decided to leave London.

He explained that he now preferred to regard his three Empire novels

> as a triptych rather than as a trilogy with each panel presenting a picture of the Empire at a different historical watershed and by their association shedding, I hope, some light on each other. I can't promise that I won't add other Imperial panels and turn it into a polyptych. (MD2)

Farrell bought a farmhouse on the remote Sheep's Head peninsula in County Cork with the intention of 'becoming Irish again'.[22] He moved there in April 1979 and set to work on finishing a short novel set in the hill station of Simla twenty years after the Indian Mutiny. It seems to have been intended as a modest sequel to *The Siege of Krishnapur* and would evidently not have been as ambitious, historical or political as his previous three books. The manuscript, untitled and consisting of an unrevised and unfinished first draft of around 50,000 words, was edited by John Spurling and posthumously published in 1981 under the title *The Hill Station*.

On 11 August 1979, four months after moving to his new home in Ireland, J. G. Farrell was fishing from some rocks on the beach below his farmhouse when he either slipped or was washed by a large wave into the sea and drowned. He was 44 years old. Farrell's body was washed ashore later the same month on the other side of Bantry Bay, and he was buried in the graveyard of St James's Church, Durrus, not far from his new home.

Of the obituaries which subsequently appeared Derek Mahon probably came closest to understanding Farrell the novelist when he wrote that 'his artistic ambitions were large. . . . He measured himself, I suspect, against the giants of modern literature; and, given the time, he might have joined them.'[23] Farrell's death also occasioned a fine and perceptive essay from Charles Palliser in the *Literary Review*. Palliser described Farrell as 'the most talented member of an otherwise disappointing generation of British novelists' and argued that his historical novels have an almost Tolstoyan objectivity which is partly due to their setting in a past whose political, economic and ideological contradictions are understood without being patronized. Farrell's characters illuminate the particular historical context in which they are caught without ever being reduced to mere representative figures.[24]

More praise for Farrell's *oeuvre* came with the posthumous publication of *The Hill Station*. Paul Theroux asserted that Farrell wrote 'in prose that is as modern as anything written today';[25] John Osborne commented, 'what a striking loss he is to the craft he pursued with massive care'.[26] Even A. N. Wilson, the only reviewer to dislike *The Hill Station*, conceded that Farrell was 'one of the outstanding novelists of his generation'.[27] Perhaps the shrewdest review came from Nicholas Shrimpton, who, noting that Farrell was a great admirer of Solzhenitsyn's *The First Circle* (1968), commented:

> Solzhenitsyn's great novel sets out to tell his fellow-countrymen who they are by giving them an image of their own forbidden past. Farrell's remarkable trilogy . . . suggests that we too, the British, will not properly understand how we live now until we make some sense of our neglected national memories.[28]

The parallel which Shrimpton draws between the intentions of both novelists is an instructive one. Farrell was an enthusiastic reader of dissident accounts of history (ranging from Solzhenitsyn to Trotsky's autobiography and N. Mandelstam's *Hope against Hope*) and his trilogy forms part of an international trend among such writers as Gabriel García Márquez, William Styron and, more recently, E. L. Doctorow towards a vigorous, aesthetically self-aware historical fiction. It is probably no coincidence that when the hero of *The Singapore Grip* ventures out into the seething backstreets of Singapore he encounters a small boy hammering on a tin drum – Farrell's homage, perhaps, to *The Tin Drum* (1959), an ambitious and massively influential fiction of historical retrieval which inaugurated Günter Grass's 'Danzig trilogy'.

V. G. Kiernan has attacked the *New Cambridge Modern History* for suffering from 'a vast lapse of vision or memory'[29] in its treatment of imperialism, and Farrell's Empire trilogy can sensibly be set alongside a number of post-war texts by socialist or Marxist historians anxious to retrieve forgotten or suppressed aspects of our history (e.g. E. P. Thompson's *The Making of the English Working Class* (1963) and *Whigs and Hunters* (1975), E. J. Hobsbawm and George Rudé's *Captain Swing* (1969) and Angus Calder's *The People's War* (1969)). Of course Farrell was writing fictional not factual historical narrative, but nevertheless, as Margaret Drabble has noted, the Empire trilogy is 'at heart political' (*HS*, p. 190). Certainly Farrell was acutely aware of the relativism of historical interpretation – something nicely summed up in the scene in *The Singapore Grip* in which Walter Blackett casually reveals the ruthless and cynical operations of his business against the native population to a reporter from the *Straits Times* who promptly converts these revelations into bland and anodyne prose.

Ultimately the politics of the Empire trilogy seem elusive and ambiguous. Victoria Glendinning has noted that 'nothing in J. G. Farrell's world was simple':

> His dislike for the tyranny and distortions of colonialism is always apparent, as is his respect for the most hopeless individual. . . . he has sympathy for those caught up in good faith in a decaying system of empire – such as the major in *Troubles*. Maybe it was this compassionate ambivalence that made him such a good writer.[30]

Farrell chose to set his mature fiction in a past where the ideological contradictions are understood, placed and 'defused by time' (MD1) as a means of illuminating what he saw as the bankrupt cultural discourse of the present. At the heart of Farrell's trilogy an anguished, embattled and perhaps unfashionable liberal humanism expresses its sense of compassion and helplessness before the dark, turbulent and ultimately tragic forces of history.

# 2

## MEN FROM ELSEWHERE

In the best ordered of lives a moment always comes when the scenery collapses. Why this and that, this woman, this job and this appetite for a future? To put it in a nutshell, why this fever for life in these legs that are going to rot? (Albert Camus, review of *Nausea*)

The title of Farrell's first novel, *A Man From Elsewhere*, points to a basic theme which was to underlie almost all his subsequent fiction, namely that of the solitary male hero who ventures out into a strange and alien environment. Sayer, Sands, Boris, the Major, Fleury and Matthew Webb – central characters in Farrell's first six novels – each leave a familiar world behind and find themselves plunged, sometimes comically, often in heroic isolation, into unknown and threatening circumstances. In the Empire trilogy the displacement becomes literal as Farrell's middle-class English characters are thrust into truly and disturbingly foreign situations. The last sentence of *A Man From Elsewhere* leaves the reader with an image of the world as a 'shining maze' (*MFE*, p. 190) and this is exactly what Farrell's characters find themselves in – labyrinths difficult to penetrate, states of confusion, lonely ordeals.

Towards the end of his career Farrell developed an inordinate dislike of *A Man From Elsewhere* and half-jokingly remarked that one of his ambitions was to buy up all surviving copies and pulp them. In 1978 he dropped the book from the list of his novels printed on the title verso of *The Singapore Grip* and it remains the only volume by Farrell never to have been re-issued. Authors not infrequently develop such antagonisms towards their earliest published work and Farrell was certainly correct in perceiving that *A Man From Elsewhere* is greatly inferior to any of his other novels. *A Man From Elsewhere* is a young man's book, serious, sombre, philosophical. It is set in France in 1961, the time that Farrell himself was living there. The plot centres on the mission of a young Communist journalist, Sayer, to uncover material suitable for destroying the reputation of a famous novelist, Regan, who is dying. Regan is an ex-Party member about to be awarded 'the Catholic Prize for World Peace' and Sayer is sent from Paris to interview the writer in the remote backwater of Saint Guilhelm, where Regan has lived for twenty years. There are rumours that Regan was a collaborator and Sayer sets to work quizzing both Regan and those who know him in an attempt to uncover the truth about some murky wartime episodes involving Regan's wife, the German commandant and some young men who were executed.

*A Man From Elsewhere* shows the strong influence of Camus, Sartre and Existentialism upon the young Farrell. His title rather baldly echoes that of Camus's *The Outsider* (1942) and the book's political concerns are more typical of French writing of the period than of current English fiction (indeed, as John Spurling has pointed out, Farrell even *looks* like a Frenchman in the carefully posed dustjacket photograph). The ambiance of Farrell's fictionalized France is that of a then-fashionable ennui and despair. When asked what she would like to do if she could choose anything at all, the young girl Monique retorts, 'Nothing . . . that's just it, there's nothing I'd like to do' (*MFE*, p. 168). This sentiment is echoed by the young actor, Simon:

> Take any moderately sensitive person of my age in a world without values and you'll find he's really up against it. It's hard to carry on when you simply don't believe in anything, when you know the next war will be the last and that there's sure to be a war. (p. 57)

Luc, the scriptwriter who has wasted his talents in the making of trashy but commercially successful movies asserts that God is dead: 'He died just the other day of bronchitis complicated by illusions of grandeur. So nobody cares, you see' (p. 77). Even Regan, the great novelist, looks back over his life and dejectedly sees 'nothing but chaos, self-delusion and fatigue' (p. 105). *A Man From Elsewhere* is a bleak cheerless book with a bleak cheerless ending and the wit, irony and charitable good humour which is so characteristic of Farrell's mature fiction is strikingly absent from this rather mordant, solemn first novel.

The interest of *A Man From Elsewhere* today lies mainly in the way it shows Farrell toying with techniques and themes later to become central to his historical novels. These include a romantically melancholy view of male-female relations (*A Man From Elsewhere* begins and ends with Sayer making his farewell to a woman), the *inertia* of Luc, later to become a major trait of Farrell's heroes, and the set-piece debates on life, culture and history. Regan represents a liberal individualist viewpoint and asserts 'take care of the means and the end will take care of itself' (p. 111), whereas Sayer is an orthodox Communist hardliner. The argument between Sayer and Regan is an old one and in part echoes the famous quarrel between Sartre and Camus after publication of *The Rebel* in 1951. *A Man From Elsewhere* is a novel of ideas, genuinely dialectical in the sense that the author abstains from siding with either party in the debate. One expects Regan to emerge the winner, since he is a novelist and Sayer a cold machine-like figure indifferent to the attractions of fiction ('For me novels confuse issues and obscure the truth rather than reveal it', he curtly remarks (p. 98)). In fact Sayer succeeds in untangling the dark secrets of Regan's past, revealing him to be not a collaborator but a man who has destroyed those who loved him most, for the sake of creating a new ideal. In their final confrontation Regan is shown to have far more in common with Sayer than the reader could have imagined was possible.

Lastly there is the all-important theme of *the body*. Farrell emphasizes the frailty and tangible physical decay of the dying Regan. There are also Gretchen's grotesque reflections upon the absurdity of human physical relations. She imagines sexual intercourse as 'a sort of eight-limbed Australian crawl' (p. 59), and on the beach looks around 'with disillusioned eyes' (p. 129), imagining how a passing seagull might interpret the sight of Sayer and herself lying below:

> She was looking at two animals of the species known as human beings lying prostrate on the sand ... They were occupied in changing a mixture of oxygen, nitrogen, and one or two other gases she could not remember offhand into carbon dioxide and water vapour. This worthy pastime seemed to occupy them exclusively, although they may have been combining it with one or two sordid digestive functions hidden from the casual observer. (pp. 129–30)

This unromantic, defamiliarizing view of human beings as slightly absurd creatures with identities determined and limited by the functioning of their bodies was later to become a trademark of Farrell's writing, and it forms the central theme of his next novel, *The Lung*. *The Lung* provides a grimly humorous account of a man in an iron lung fighting his way back to health in the company of some comically eccentric fellow patients and a desirable young nurse. The human body as a fragile, vulnerable organism is an omnipresent motif. The novel's protagonist, Martin Sands, contracts polio and has to spend months in hospital. He makes friends with a young girl, Monica, only to learn later that she is dying from leukaemia. At the end of the book we are reminded that inside the face of the attractive nurse lies a rotting tooth.

Severe as they are, Sands's problems are not simply physical. He is another outsider figure, 'suffocated by the drapings of indifference that hung on every aspect of his life like sodden garments' (*L*, p. 199). He finds it hard to communicate with others; his marriage has broken up; he has abandoned his job as a reporter, disgusted by it. From being an alienated member of the world of the healthy Sands is abruptly transported to an enclosed community of the sick, where his condition merely worsens. Sands is consumed by world-weariness. He ceaselessly contemplates the decay and inevitable death of all living things and grimly reflects:

Most intelligent people end up by becoming an expert on something, but what I can't understand is how they manage to persuade themselves in the first place that these things are important. Once persuaded, once you've managed to slink over the barrier of absurdity I see, of course, that they become an agreeable way of passing the time but . . . What have they to do with being alive? (p. 166)

Sex, Sands decides, provides a partial palliative of his over-reaching *Angst*, and he attains redemption of a sort by seducing Marigold, his nurse (who, by a bizarre coincidence, also happens to be his stepdaughter). The future prospects for their relationship seem bleak, particularly since Sands's motives for pursuing her veer uncertainly from lust to boredom to competition with another patient. The flip cynicism of the final sentences ('I married my ex-stepdaughter and we had ten children and lived happily ever after. It was just terrible' (p. 207)) underline Sands's sardonic inability to take anything seriously except the brute facts of physical decay and extinction.

*The Lung* is a more ambitious novel than *A Man From Elsewhere* and is prefaced by portentous epigraphs from Tolstoy and A. Landsborough Thomson indicating how the human spirit is dragged down by the desires and needs of the flesh. In between writing his first and second novels Farrell had evidently discovered Malcolm Lowry's *Under the Volcano* (1947) and the first three chapters of *The Lung* clearly demonstrate Lowry's intoxicating influence. Martin Sands, drunk, fortyish, wearer of dark glasses, prey to unnerving hallucinations and desiring only to go home 'where he could vomit away in peace, undisturbed by other people's good intentions' (*L*, p. 43) is all too visibly a reincarnation of Lowry's legendary hero, the Consul. But though *The Lung* is crammed with jokes and literary allusions the tone of the narrative is uneven and Farrell fails to sustain the kind of tragic irony which underpins Lowry's masterpiece. The handling of the theme of disease and hospitalization in *The Lung* is uncertain. The documentary realism of the scenes which focus on Sands's bleakly painful physical incapacity are juxtaposed rather uneasily with the wildly unrealistic comic scenes involving Exmoore, Rivers and Harris. Much of the novel (again imitating Lowry) takes place inside Sands's mind and consists of autobiographical fragments and surrealistic fantasies. Many of these fantasies are extremely funny, but they risk the charge of self-indulgence (as, typically, in the case of the tiger swallowed by the lungfish: 'Only presence of mind and a king-size box of laxative tablets available from all good chemists saved him from unpleasant fate' (p. 68)).

Farrell had yet to discover suitable narrative material which would enable him convincingly to relate a melancholy hero with the world at large using a style in which realism merged imperceptibly into fantasy. The problems which arise in *The Lung* out of the author's own too-close identification with the protagonist are present in Farrell's next novel, *A Girl in the Head*. The plot concerns the comic misadventures of Count Boris Slattery, 'a gaunt man with receding hair' (*GIH*, p. 33), in the dull, provincial seaside resort of Maidenhair Bay, 'the cemetery of all initiative and endeavour' (p. 15). Boris (who it seems may not really be a Polish Count at all but simply Mick Slattery, a smooth-talking Irishman from Limerick) is a penniless wanderer who has found refuge by marrying into the Dongeon family. His relationship with his wife, Flower, has broken down and he spends his time behaving eccentrically and wandering aimlessly around Maidenhair Bay involving himself in unfortunate situations.

Boris (a name possibly intended to evoke comic associations with the screen actor Boris Karloff, famous for his impersonations of Frankenstein's shambling monster) bears a number of similarities to Martin Sands. Like Sands he is haunted by thoughts of death and consumed by a sense of the absurdity and worthlessness of existence. Boris, like Sands, also suffers from ill-health and the novel begins with his suffering a mild heart attack and being conveyed to a nearby hospital. There are further echoes of *Under the Volcano*: Boris wears dark glasses,

41

carries a silver flask of brandy around with him, is followed by a stray dog and is unnerved by a sunflower staring at him. The characters whom Farrell intends to be the most sympathetic are those who, like Lowry's Consul, have seen through the illusions which sustain the mass of mankind. At the end of *The Lung* Exmoore (whose *real* name is Moore) waits by the hospital gates, slashing at some nettles with a silver-knobbed cane, 'The picture of [a] decadent aristocrat' (*L*, p. 205). Exmoore explains how he came to abandon religion and the pulpit ('It's just that I realised that I wanted them to love *me*, not God. I didn't give a damn about God' (*L*, p. 206)). Boris is largely a reincarnation of Exmoore and Sands, and his despairing speech to Flower which terminates the narrative echoes (even syntactically) the hesitancy and weary resignation of Exmoore's final words.

The theme of despair is underlined in *A Girl in the Head* by the appearance of Cohen, the drunken ex-doctor. Cohen has given up medicine, convinced that human beings are nothing more than machines. Boris attempts to cling to some sustaining illusion and, disagreeing with Cohen, puts his faith in young love. His hopes that a relationship will blossom between the shy, inexperienced Alessandro and Inez are brutally shattered when he encounters Inez copulating with his lecherous brother-in-law, Maurice. Shortly afterwards Boris cuts down the sycamore tree in the garden, an implicit symbol of himself.

Farrell had evidently been enthusiastically reading Nabokov around the time he wrote *A Girl in the Head*. Count Boris Slattery's extravagant aristocratic ancestry clearly owes much to Nabokov, as does Farrell's use of odd and absurd names. Farrell's title points to Nabokov's *Lolita* (1955) – the classic account of 'a girl in the head' – but neither Inez nor Boris's old flame Ylva possess his imagination with anything like the monstrous, obsessive intensity of Humbert Humbert's enchantment by a 'mythopoeic nymphet'.[31]

After *A Girl in the Head* Farrell abandoned comic novels, English settings and the contemporary period. In later years Farrell looked back upon his first three novels with some

dissatisfaction, describing them as mere 'casting around' (GB)
— the efforts of a young writer in search of a theme and not yet
finding it. Farrell did however subsequently write one more
piece of comic fiction, 'The Pussycat Who Fell in Love with the
Suitcase', his only published story. It is a bizarre, eccentric
piece narrated in the intimate tone of voice which is such a
striking feature of the Empire trilogy. The story concerns a cat
named Rameses, who is a shop-steward in a peppermint
factory. One day Rameses comes home to find a suitcase in the
middle of his bedroom floor. Rameses falls head-over-heels in
love with the suitcase, which responds with a disdainful,
indifferent silence. The lovelorn cat absents himself from the
factory and industrial disputes soon bring chaos to the town.
The Mayor therefore hides a tape-recorder in the case so that
every five minutes it tells Rameses it loves him.

> The next day Rameses was back at the peppermint factory
> and soon everything was running smoothly again in our
> town. How pleased all the townspeople were that they no
> longer had to eat raw peppermints. And Rameses seemed
> quite happy too. Pretty soon he was leading exactly the same
> life as he had before. After a few weeks he was to be seen
> back in the pub drinking peppermint beer as he always had
> done and, one evening, he told one of his friends that he was
> not as much in love with the suitcase as everybody thought.
> Although, of course, he agreed that the suitcase had a
> beautiful body, he explained to his friends, she was inclined
> to be clinging and to be frank, was not all that interesting to
> talk to. But then you can't have everything, can you?
> One of these days I expect the Mayor will forget to change
> the batteries and the suitcase will stop telling Rameses that it
> loves him. But I doubt if Rameses will ever notice. He's quite
> affectionate towards the suitcase, however, and I'm quite
> sure they will both live happily ever after, the way people do.
> (*P*, p. 10)

Beneath the light comedy one can detect a continuity with
the gloomy view of human relations which Sands and Boris

subscribe to. It is a chilling, ironic view of human relationships and one which Farrell was to elaborate very much more compellingly in his comically entertaining but ultimately dark, sombre and tragic Empire trilogy.

## 3

## THE SENSE OF AN ENDING

> They lived like blind men in a large room, aware only of what came in contact with them (and of that only imperfectly), but unable to see the general aspect of things. (Joseph Conrad, 'An Outpost of Progress')

*Troubles*, arguably Farrell's masterpiece, has certain features in common with two works he particularly admired, Conrad's *Heart of Darkness* (1899) and Malcolm Lowry's *Under the Volcano* (1947). *Troubles* is one of those texts which are grounded in a naturalistic world but which are open to numerous other dimensions and nuances of meaning. In *Troubles* Farrell created, like Conrad and Lowry, a unique fictional world narrated in a realistic mode which constantly and subtly metamorphoses into other styles and types of narrative, including the fairy tale, myth, fantasy, symbolism and parody.

At its most immediately engaging, *Troubles* tells the tragicomic tale of Major Brendan Archer's prolonged sojourn in Ireland, where he blunderingly pursues two women, the first of whom unexpectedly dies and the second of whom is secretly carrying on an affair with another man. The Major, an English gentleman, is a melancholy, passive character, hopelessly out of his element in Ireland. Invited to stay at the vast, crumbling Majestic Hotel, owned by Edward Spencer, his fiancée's father, he finds himself trapped in a soporific labyrinth, unable to escape. The hotel occupies a lonely, isolated site in County Wexford, on the southeast coast of Ireland. It was, we learn, built during the high noon of the British Empire and is truly representative of the old order. It is visibly in an advanced state of decay. The gates which once stood at the entrance are no longer there. The porter's lodge is overgrown and its windows are smashed. The hotel itself is like a mausoleum, dark and dusty, containing – as the Major discovers to his horror on his first night – rotting flesh.

A note of ironic detachment is struck from the first page. The cool retrospective opening sentences examine the passing of the Majestic from the perspective of an unidentified present (implicitly the late 1960s, when the book was written). There is a great emphasis on time, without specifying any particular year or period: 'In those days. . . . At that time. . . . now . . . years ago . . . a few years later still . . . by that time . . .' (*T*, p. 9). This anticipates the chronology of the rest of the novel, where life at the Majestic takes on a curiously timeless, elusive, indefinable quality (although the novel is scattered with contemporary newspaper reports *very few of them are dated*), and new sections of the narrative typically begin 'One day' or 'At about this time'. There are no chapter divisions in *Troubles*, giving the impression of a continuum. The narrative is cast in the form of two lengthy unbroken sections of around 200 pages, set in July 1919–summer 1920 and autumn 1920–July 1921 respectively. The book (like the House of Usher) is thus split in two, fissured. Part One ends with Captain Bolton eating the rose and Edward relating how the official in Dublin Castle was drunk: both signify the end. Bolton steals Sarah from Edward and the Major, and the administration in Dublin will not rule for very much longer.

As in *Under the Volcano* the opening pages of *Troubles* are set long after the events which are to follow. A dry, impersonal, factual voice records the oblivion into which the Majestic has disappeared. In the second paragraph a chattier, more engaging style of voice takes over, assuring the reader that the ruins of the hotel may still be seen. Indeed, the reader is informed that if s/he were to visit the site then s/he, like the narrator, could disinter small pools of crystal: 'Pick them up and they separate in your hand into the cloudy droplets that formed them' (*T*, p. 10).

There is a curious kind of double-exposure present in the novel, since in setting the scene the narrator mimics the actions of the Major at the very end of the book. Both the Major (in July 1921) and the narrator (in the late 1960s) pay a melancholy visit to the Majestic's charred remains, still miraculously visible half a century after the fire. To the narrator the fire 'hardly mattered' (p. 10) and to the Major the hotel's remains are 'quite insignificant' (p. 446). The authority of this narrative voice is a sham, however. The Majestic hotel never existed and Kilnalough cannot be found on any map of Ireland for the simple reason that Farrell invented it ('Kilnalough' is derived from Gaelic and means 'church or burial place of the lake'). The ruins of the Majestic, like Lowry's Quauhnahuac, exist nowhere other than as words on a printed page.

Farrell's prose persuades us otherwise. The Majestic is a vividly convincing place, half-real, half-dream. When the Major first arrives at the hotel it seems as if he has come to a stagnant, timeless world. He comes to claim his bride like the Prince in search of the Sleeping Beauty, encountering a mysterious turreted hotel which greatly resembles the overgrown, enchanted castle of the fairy story. Cobwebs billow from the ceilings, banisters are garnished with spiders' webs, iron balconies rust, dogs and cats lie about the building asleep in unexpected places. The fairy story parallels soon turn sour, however. Angela, the Major's fiancée, appears older than he had been expecting and seems pallid, fatigued and fretful. Later, when Angela is dead, the Major is belatedly informed by her family that she had leukaemia.

The Major in fact turns out to be less like a fairy-tale prince than Alice in Wonderland, venturing with perplexed eyes through a zany and incomprehensible domain of extraordinary occurrences. There are some continuities between the Major and Farrell's previous heroes. He is not a well man, having spent some time in hospital, and he is consumed by a brooding sense of apathy and indifference towards society. Unlike the other Farrell outsiders, however, the Major can truly be said to have earned his *Angst*, having served in the trenches during the First World War. The Major is an altogether credible figure; he has far more density than Farrell's previous protagonists and his melancholia seems to spring naturally from his character rather than being, as Boris's is, histrionic. The Major arrives at the Majestic 'with drugged eyes' (p. 26) and the narrative that follows has a dreamy, hallucinatory quality that has sometimes been compared with Mervyn Peake's fantastic world of Gormenghast. Margaret Drabble has noted that 'There are few writers who have made such pervasive use of the emotion of bewilderment' as Farrell: 'Confused, puzzled, surprised, doubtful, uncertain, hesitating, depressed – these are words that appear with haunting regularity' (*HS*, pp. 188–9). The Major is perhaps the most baffled of all Farrell's characters. Major events of the plot lie outside his knowledge: none of the Spencers tells him that Angela has leukaemia, he remains ignorant of Sarah's physical relationship with Edward until the traumatic night that their affair comes to an end, and he is unaware of Sarah's feelings for Bolton and is stunned by the news that she has run off to Dublin with him. His bewilderment is reminiscent of Alice's: like her he is the passive victim of a mad, confusing surrealistic world where he never seems to win.

The Majestic is a microcosm of Ireland: to enter it is to sink into an enervating swamp of dreams, illusions and apathetic stagnation. It is an Ireland familiar from that Anglo-Irish comic classic *The Irish R.M.* (1928). Somerville and Ross portray *their* Major as the victim of an endless melancholy cycle of trivial events in a timeless provincial world:

> The well-known routine followed; the long and airless day in the court-house, the roar of battle of the rival solicitors, the wearisome iteration of drunks and trespasses, the intricacies of family feuds; the stodgy and solitary dinner at the hotel, followed by the evening in the arid smoking-room, the stale politics of its habitués, the stagnant pessimism of the proprietor, the same thing over again next day and the day after.[32]

For Farrell's Major life is one long round of grotesque or discomforting situations. His romantic farewell to Angela in

1916 occurred, we learn, while he had his hand accidentally pressed upon a cactus, 'which had rendered many of his parting words insincere' (*T*, p. 12). Upon first arriving at the hotel the Major is invited by his prospective father-in-law to join in a hunt for trespassers in the grounds, inspiring the Major to reflect that 'he had no intention of shooting anyone on his first day in Ireland if he could possibly avoid it' (p. 27). This comic world is familiar from Somerville and Ross, but Farrell's comedy has an altogether harder, darker edge.

At first the Major resists his inevitable fate: 'like a man struggling to retain his consciousness as he inhales the first fumes of chloroform, he had not yet allowed himself to surrender to the country's vast and narcotic inertia' (p. 42). But the Major suffers from weariness and apathy (the result of his wartime experiences) before he even arrives in Ireland, and consequently his resistance to its drowsy, soporific atmosphere is shortlived.

The lengthy description of the Majestic given in the novel's opening pages evokes a building which seems as much the fabric of a dream as a structure of brick and plaster. Farrell emphasizes its almost ungraspable larger-than-life size: the gateposts are *massive*, the foliage is *impenetrable*, there are the remains of *enormous* iron hinges on the gateposts, each of which is surmounted by a *great* stone ball:

> they reached the park over which loomed the dark mass of the hotel. The size of the place astonished the Major. As they approached he looked up at the great turreted wall hanging over them and tried to count the balconies and windows. (p. 18)

Arriving at the hotel the Major finds himself alone, faced by a 'massive' (p. 19) front door beyond which lies a 'vast flowing staircase' (Ibid.). Inside, from 'an immensely long chain' (Ibid.), hangs 'a great glass chandelier' (p. 20).

There are hints that the Majestic exists at an odd angle to reality: the ancient pendulum clock above the reception desk shows the wrong time (later it stops altogether) and on each stone ball on the hotel gateposts 'a rain-polished stone crown was perched slightly askew, lending the gateposts a drunken, ridiculous air, like solemn men in paper hats' (p. 18). Significantly, the incongruous, asymmetrical topsy-turvy world of the Majestic is surrounded by 'dead pines leaning here and there at odd angles' (p. 9).

The hotel is a shadowy, dreamlike, twilight zone of 'gloomy carpeted corridors' (p. 19), 'gloomy foliage' (p. 20), containing 'a vast, shadowy cavern' with 'a distant murky skylight' (Ibid.) It can scarcely be a coincidence that as soon as the Major plunges into the gloomy interior of the Majestic he at once finds himself taking part in a tea party every bit as whimsical and strange as the Mad Hatter's (Dr Ryan even bears a certain resemblance to the Dormouse). That the Major has entered a dreamland is ironically underlined later in the novel: on the night of the ball when the besotted Major finally decides to propose to Sarah the sound of the orchestra playing 'Dreamland Lover' grows louder in his ears. He is himself a 'dreamland lover', engaged in the vain pursuit of elusive and opaque dream women.

Beneath the humour and grotesquerie lies only tragedy, however. Farrell's Ireland is a blighted Eden, and the apples in the hotel's orchard are 'shrivelled and bitter' (p. 31). When Adam meets Eve the encounter is grotesque and ominous:

> Coming to the edge of the orchard at a point where the drive touched it at a tangent, the Major saw a girl in a wheelchair. She was holding up two heavy walking-sticks and trying to use them as pincers to grasp a large green apple that hung out of her reach. Ripon hesitated when he saw her and whispered 'Oh Lord, she's seen us. She's absolutely poisonous.' (p. 32)

*Troubles* begins, then, by evoking a fantastic, unreal world redolent of myth and fairy tales. But as the narrative progresses the timeless world of the Majestic hotel, like that of Ireland itself, is gradually impinged upon by the timebound outside world. Beyond the human comedy played out in the foreground lies the struggle for Irish independence, a tragicomedy which, like the goings-on inside the Majestic, is frequently both farcical and grotesque. As the 'troubles' move closer to the Majestic the Major and the other occupants are gradually diverted from their own domestic and emotional troubles. The forces of twentieth-century history which are sweeping away the old order are starkly suggested by the press reports in the Major's newspaper for 1 July 1919. Bolshevism still thrives in Russia, militant Republicanism is at work in Ireland. Although at the sight of these press stories the Major merely yawns and dozes off he is destined to discover that not even he is immune from the force of historical change.

*Troubles* takes its title from the popular phrase 'the troubles', traditionally taken to refer to the first Irish civil war of 1919–21 but now sometimes used in connection with the civil unrest which began in Northern Ireland in 1968 and which has continued to the present day. The novel is set over a precise two-year period, from July 1919 to July 1921. When the Major first arrives in Ireland the civil war is still in its early stages. At this time Ireland was part of the United Kingdom and governed by the English from Dublin Castle. In January 1919 the Irish Republican Army (or IRA) was formed and began a guerilla war against the English administration. The historian A. J. P. Taylor has commented:

> The 'troubles', as they were called, had a topsy-turvy character. The I.R.A., though stigmatized as rebels, fought in the name of an existing republic against the British 'invaders'. The British, though claiming to maintain order, were fighting to recover an authority which they had already lost.[33]

The Major's sojourn in Ireland coincides with the worst phase of the civil war, during which the British brought in the Black and Tans and then the 'Auxis', or Auxiliary Division, 'men with a taste for fighting and brutality, who became an autonomous terror squad'.[34] *Troubles* ends in July 1921, the month that a truce was signed which ended this period of fighting and which eventually resulted in the establishment of the Irish Free State.

*Troubles* is a novel, not a history book, and Farrell does little to inform the reader about the complicated developments of modern Irish history. His characters are not involved in the major historical events of the 'troubles' (such as the infamous burning-down of Cork by the Black and Tans) but perceive them from a distance, usually through the unreliable medium of press reports in newspapers unsympathetic to the Republican cause. The reader who knows little about Irish history is likely to share the Major's bafflement about what exactly is going on. History is represented as a dimly understood force which moves sluggishly towards the incomprehending and indifferent inhabitants of the Majestic, only at the end engulfing their world, dispossessing them and driving them out.

Farrell's use of history is dramatic rather than didactic. The Major goes to stay among the Anglo-Irish who, as Protestants, are on the other side of the religious divide to the majority Catholic population and are aligned with the forces of conservative inertia. The case for change is made negatively, through the prejudice and irrationality of the Anglo-Irish, and the Republican viewpoint is only obliquely present in the novel.

The Major is a good-natured, clumsy, myopic individual and once ensconced at the Majestic he becomes involved in a long sequence of misunderstandings and deceptions which symbolize the divided condition of Ireland. No one tells him about Angela's leukaemia and when he enquires about her medical state the doctor thinks he is referring to Sarah and gives him a misleadingly encouraging prognosis. Later, Sarah flirts with the Major while secretly maintaining a liaison with Edward Spencer, who lies to the Major about the couple's trip to Dublin. The Major, meanwhile, is a reluctant witness to Ripon's deception of both his father and his wife. Appropriately, the generator at the hotel has failed and there is no electricity. The hotel is consequently an area of twilight and shadows, a vast dark maze in which no one ever quite seems to know what anyone else is up to.

The Major finds the Irish servants incomprehensible and at times literally unintelligible:

> 'What's all this?' he demanded sternly. 'The devil? You must speak plainly and slowly. I don't understand you.'
>
> But the cook plunged on faster than ever, repeating the same mysterious phrases again and again while the Major tried in vain to fit them into some coherent pattern. Could she be speaking Irish? Or was it merely her defective palate, abetted, he suspected, by the absence of teeth? (pp. 366–7)

In fact the visitor whose arrival at the hotel has so terrified the cook turns out not to be the devil but Sarah's father, Mr Devlin. He, in turn, is 'incapable of speaking straight' (p. 367).

In a world of rigidly defined positions, ranging from Catholic nationalism to Unionist reaction, it is the Major who occupies the middle ground and who half-heartedly endeavours to understand the turmoil into which he has unwittingly descended. At first the Major is merely baffled by accounts in the press of reprisals which have been carried out against those Irish men and women who are servants of the British government or who fraternize with British troops. Gradually, however, the Major learns to discard many of his received opinions as an Englishman. Later, as he witnesses at first hand the sufferings and misery of the Irish peasantry, he dimly begins to comprehend the forces pressing for Irish independence. As a muddled liberal, however, the Major has no idea how to come to terms with the poverty and hunger he witnesses all around him – something underlined by his sympathetic but utterly inadequate gesture of handing out chocolate bars to the ragged, famished children he meets while out walking.

The individuals who are fighting for change remain on the sidelines, sinister figures flitting about on the peripheries. When the IRA finally comes to abduct the Major its representatives remain faceless and voiceless, nothing more than 'a convulsion of the shadows' (p. 434). The only character in *Troubles* who is directly involved in violent struggle against the Anglo-Irish is Murphy, a grotesque creature of the shadows, whose subversive politics are largely a matter of hints and whispers and whose motives are obscure. When the empty-headed Unionist braggart Boy O'Neill remarks that the Auxiliaries will give the 'Shinners' something to think about, the Major coldly and percipiently retorts that the cure may be as bad as the disease. The Major's own first-hand experience of Ireland advances his understanding of the situation enormously and yet in the end his liberalism proves inadequate to the situation. The forces which he cannot comprehend overwhelm him (almost literally at the end of the novel) and he relapses into a weary impatience:

> presently the Major's sense of shock and dismay over the degeneration of British justice evaporated, leaving only a sediment of contempt and indifference. After all, if one lot was as bad as the other why should anyone care. 'Let them sort it out for themselves.' (p. 244)

At the end, when Edward kills a Sinn Feiner, the Major lucidly analyses the muddle of vengeful motives which underlie his brutal action. As he explains to Dr Ryan, 'The poor boy was the victim of a private hatred and despair' (p. 419). But a short while later, just when it seems that the Major's compassionate understanding marks a real development in his character, he relapses once more into a spasm of weary disgust, angrily shouting that the youth got what he deserved.

The Major's first day at the Majestic involves him in a sequence of comic episodes which might easily have come out of Somerville and Ross. But his day ends on a dark, sinister, grotesque note when he identifies the source of a sweetish, curious smell in his room:

> A small cupboard stood beside the bed. He wrenched open the door. On the top shelf there was nothing. On the bottom shelf was a chamber-pot and in the chamber-pot was a

decaying object crawling with white maggots. From the middle of this object a large eye, bluish and corrupt, gazed up at the Major, who scarcely had time to reach the bathroom before he began to vomit brown soup and steamed bacon and cabbage. (pp. 43–4)

There is nothing in Somerville and Ross like *that*. This festering object turns out to be a rotting sheep's head but it is in the nature of Farrell's fictional universe that the object is charged with significance. Decay and concealment are emblematic of the Irish body politic: beneath the whimsy and comedy other, uglier forces are stirring. Although only about fifteen years separate the periods in which *The Irish R.M.* and *Troubles* are set, the worlds of Major Sinclair Yeates and Major Brendan Archer are far removed in mood. The comedy in Farrell's version of the Irish condition is tempered by the rising tide of dissent and unrest as the civil war moves towards its apogee. The great Autumn storm which begins to blow in Part Two – 'a high wind, almost a gale, howling over the countryside' (p. 235) – is a symbolic storm, redolent of the uncontrollable passions which have been aroused.

As if to underscore the difference between his Ireland and that of Somerville and Ross, Farrell includes a comic episode reminiscent of *The Irish R.M.* but with a sombre conclusion. When Father O'Meara, who is secretly giving Ripon devotional instruction, is thrown off his bicycle by the mischievous twins, a farcical situation which threatens to get completely out of hand is terminated by a certain contemporary and distinctly unwhimsical reality:

It was a matter for the police, no doubt about it. Charges of assault were prepared for the R.M., together with counter-charges of trespass (Ripon having assured his father that the priest was nothing to do with him) and theft (some apples had been stripped from trees in the orchard). Other charges were being considered and had there been a magistrate to hear them this sudden sprouting of litigation might have grown so dense and confusing as to become, inside a few days, entirely beyond resolution. But there wasn't. This representative of the foreign oppressor had received a number of menacing letters from the I.R.A. and had wisely retired. (p. 133)

Later, we learn of the disappearance of an RM who, after reprisals are threatened, is dug up and left in a coffin on a railway line. The comedy wears thin in such circumstances and even the good-natured Major is driven bitterly to reflect that 'He hated the Irish' (p. 265).

*Trouble*, a word which is repeated on numerous occasions and in a variety of contexts throughout the novel, is what menaces individuals and empires alike. The novel provides the overture to Farrell's trilogy, for, as the Major gloomily acknowledges, 'there had always been some corner of the Empire where his Majesty's subjects were causing trouble' (p. 215). The disturbances in the body politic are global, as the press reports make clear. We hear of unrest in India, race riots in Chicago, civil war in Russia, rebellion in Mesopotamia. There is even a sombre and uncannily accurate prophecy of another world war: De Valera is reported as having warned that the Versailles peace settlement has nominally ended one war but created the prospect of twenty new ones. Typically, 'the Major . . . merely yawned at this dire prediction' (p. 15).

In *A Girl in the Head* Boris feels that there has to be a connection between his own illness and certain external events:

This girl whom he had never met, the transience of life, the passing of summer without her, the sudden collapse of his own health – all these things gradually melted into each other and fused in his mind as if they had some direct though concealed link. (*GIH*, p. 8)

Although such contingencies assume 'a strange significance' (*GIH*, p. 8) for Boris he is unable to identify what exactly that significance is. In *Troubles* the transience of life and the collapse of health are implicitly connected to the condition of Ireland and of the Empire.

The Major comes to Ireland straight from a long stay in hospital, with 'a bitter weary expression in his eyes' (*T*, p. 14), evidently still suffering from depression and nervous exhaustion. His fiancée, Angela, is dying of leukaemia, and after her death the Major falls in love with Sarah, who is a semi-cripple and suffers from a mysterious, never identified sickness. Meanwhile, back in London, the Major's aunt experiences a series of haemorrhages and expires. The physical decay of the living representatives of the old order is, in other words, tangibly present. Angela, with unselfconscious irony, provides the Major with a full account of the dental work which her family has required. We learn that her mother died of an embolism on St Swithun's Day, 1910 (St Swithun's Day falls in July, the month that *Troubles* begins and ends in, and St Swithun gloomily requested to be buried in the open, where passers-by could walk upon his grave and the rain fall upon it. By tradition if it rains on St Swithun's Day it will rain also for the following forty days. Details like this link up with the Gaelic derivation of Kilnalough as a place of burial and reinforce Farrell's symbolic landscape). The Unionist bigot Boy O'Neill is ill with cancer, while Mr Noonan — Edward Spencer's Catholic *alter ego* — suffers from chest trouble and high blood pressure.

The sickest character in *Troubles* is the Majestic itself. At the start of the novel the hotel is described in terms of a living organism, with the guests occupying a biologically beneficial role:

> the rooms they had been staying in for twenty years were dotted here and there over that immense building and, though whole wings and corners of it might be dead and decaying, there would still be a throbbing cell of life on this floor or that which had to be maintained. (p. 11)

The decaying condition of the hotel is immediately apparent to the Major upon his first arrival. The palms have burst out of their wooden tubs and grown up to the skylight, while areas of mould sustain rubber plants, ferns, elephant grass and creepers. This proliferating foliage inside the Majestic at first seems romantically exotic but is actually charged with sinister significance. Metaphorically (the disease is never explicitly identified) the Majestic has cancer. In *Illness as Metaphor* Susan Sontag points to an early definition of cancer as 'Anything that frets, corrodes, corrupts, or consumes slowly and secretly'[35] and explores some of the implications of this figurative language:

> In cancer, the patient is 'invaded' by alien cells, which multiply, causing an atrophy or blockage of bodily functions. . . . Metaphorically, cancer is not so much a disease of time as a disease or pathology of space. Its principal metaphors refer to topography (cancer 'spreads' or 'proliferates' or is 'diffused').[36]

An immense structure like the Majestic is ideally suited to the elaboration of topographical metaphors. As Patrick Skene Catling has noted, 'One of the many imaginative and technical marvels of the novel is that the metaphor of the Majestic is sustained and continually developed and embellished throughout.'[37] When Sarah demands to know from the Major what has been *going on* at the Majestic during her absence he is lost for words, but her question immediately takes on an unintended irony. The answer, it seems, is *growth* – but growth of a cancerous kind, bringing decay and collapse:

> 'Take a look at this.' Grasping a heavy plush sofa that stood in the middle of the room beside a table of warped walnut, he dragged it aside. Beneath, the wooden blocks of parquet flooring bulged ominously upward like a giant abscess. Something was trying to force its way up through the floor.
>
> 'Good heavens! What is it?'
>
> The Major knelt and removed three or four of the blocks to reveal a white, hairy wrist.
>
> 'It's a root. God only knows where it comes from: probably from the Palm Court – one of those wretched tropical things.' (p. 274)

Although the Major is disturbed by his discovery ('One shudders to think what it may be doing to the foundations' he reflects (p. 274)), Sarah finds it all rather amusing. Soon these two febrile semi-invalids have invented 'hunt the bulge', an entertainment of ominous significance:

They set off immediately, walking from one room to the next, along corridors, upstairs and downstairs. In no time this looking for bulges became a marvellous game. They spotted bulges on the walls and floor and even on the ceiling. 'Bulge!' Sarah would cry gaily and point at some offending surface. And then the Major would have to get down on his hands and knees or place his cheek against a cold wall and squint along it in order to adjudicate. Although a number of these bulges proved imaginary, once one started looking for them at the Majestic there was no shortage of genuine ones. (pp. 274–5)

The Majestic in fact is very sick indeed and this malignantly spreading vegetation becomes increasingly visible as the novel progresses. The metaphor also carries some political overtones. Ireland, in a sense, is reclaiming her own, subverting the superimposed structure of British rule and the Anglo-Irish ascendancy. The growth of an alien and uncontrollable vegetation at the Majestic runs parallel to the growth of militant Irish nationalism – something which through British or Anglo-Irish eyes is equally alien, equally beyond control. The ivy 'advancing like a green epidemic over the outside walls' (p. 287) heralds the arrival of Sinn Fein; the Majestic's condition is near-terminal.

The fall of the house of Spencer echoes one of Edgar Allan Poe's most famous stories in its association of structural and bodily decay. Poe's House of Usher is a rotten, extensively decayed building isolated in a desolate landscape and inhabited by the diseased Lady Madeline and her 'cadaverously wan'[38] twin brother. Although the narrator meets Madeline on the evening of his arrival at the house she thereafter takes to her bed and he does not see her again, something which Farrell seems to have adopted in his presentation of Angela and the Major. In Poe's fictional universe the 'acute bodily illness'[39] of Roderick Usher expresses a sickness of the psyche which is refracted in the fissured, discoloured house and the grey, barren, vacant landscape that surrounds it. The Majestic hotel, like the House of Usher, is ineluctably doomed and collapses into ruins at the end of the narrative. But *Troubles*, though sometimes described as Gothic, and while it makes use of some of the properties of this genre, conveys the idea of decay and sickness in a rather different sense from Poe. Farrell is interested in tangible physical decay rather than disorders of the psyche and the atmosphere at the Majestic too often dissolves into comedy or irony ever to seem chilling or frightening. The claim which is sometimes made that the Majestic's fiery end is a reworking of a Gothic convention rather overlooks the fact that arson attacks on large properties owned by the Anglo-Irish gentry were commonplace at this period in Irish history (Elizabeth Bowen's *The Last September* (1927), which is also set against the background of the troubles, ends with the great house Danielstown burning to the ground).

Farrell's use of illness as metaphor overlaps and merges with the novel's concurrent theme of the tragic vulnerability and brevity of human life. *Troubles* is a death-haunted novel which never lets us forget the terrible frailty of the human body. Dr Ryan, a decrepit old man, is the spokesman for this tragic vision of life which lies at the heart of the novel. The doctor insists that 'People are insubstantial. . . . They are with us for a while and then they disappear and there is nothing to be done about it' (p. 154), and after Angela's death he gloomily informs her father that 'a person is only a very temporary and makeshift affair. . . . [Angela] even at the height of her youth and health was temporary and insubstantial because . . . people are insubstantial. They really do not ever last. . . . They never last' (pp. 154–5).

Decay is everywhere in *Troubles*: in society, in the structure of the hotel, in the bodies of animals and human beings. The twins' names remind us that *Troubles* is a book with Faith and

Charity but no Hope. One of the central tragic statements of the novel occurs in a marvellous comic scene where the Major and Dr Ryan irritably prepare together an almost inedible Christmas dinner. The doctor shuffles to and from the lavatory, reiterating that life 'is a fugitive affair at best' (p. 307). Upon his second return from the lavatory Dr Ryan reiterates his favourite idea:

> Strange, said the doctor coming back, to think that a beautiful woman who seemed like a solid thing, solid as granite, was really no more solid than a flaring match, a burst of flame, darkness before and darkness after. . . . People are insubstantial, they never last. (p. 307)

Dr Ryan's melancholy account of the human condition is really a restatement of some famous lines from the Book of Job which Farrell was subsequently to quote in his next novel, *The Siege of Krishnapur*: 'Man that is born of woman, is of few days, and full of trouble: – He cometh forth like a flower, and is cut down; he fleeth also as a shadow, and continueth not' (Job 14:1, 2). The reader's last sight of Edward is of him surveying his grounds for one last time before going into exile, and remarking 'I remember the day we brought Angie home in the snow. She was only a baby. It hardly seems any time at all' (p. 430). This perfectly expresses the quiet, subdued tragic vision of *Troubles*. Tragedy as a mode often involves or climaxes in spectacular acts of violence but Farrell's concern in this novel is more with the humdrum and everyday.

Farrell's tragic vision is traditional rather than modern. The gaunt figure of Murphy, the destroyer, is glimpsed carrying a scythe like Death in a medieval illustration. The Majestic hotel is itself a place of darkness, 'infernally dark' (p. 158), swathed in the presence of death. Farrell's characters, particularly Murphy, repeatedly *materialize* out of the shadows and then *fade* or *melt back into the darkness*. Murphy is reminiscent of Wang, another disloyal servant, in Conrad's *Victory* (1915). *Victory*, like *Troubles*, evokes a decaying, cut-off world doomed to be destroyed by the intrusion of alien outside forces.

61

Both novels are informed by a melancholy sense of the futility of human endeavour and both climax with a fiery holocaust.

It is ironic that though a beautiful woman seems, in Dr Ryan's words, 'like a solid thing, solid as granite' (p. 307), the only woman the Major succeeds in bringing back with him from Ireland is a 'lady of white marble' (p. 446) – namely, the hotel's statue of Venus. In part this testifies to the failure of the Major's human relationships. His notion of love is too idealized for actual living women. He has been blind to Angela's empty snobbery (clearly she fell in love less with the Major as an individual than as a fashionable war hero, an officer at the front), and he understands Sarah even less. Sarah, it appears, needs and desires a man who is even more violent and abrasive than she is herself, and finds him in Captain Bolton, whose seduction of her is symbolized by the scene in which he devours a rose, thorns and all, in front of the horrified old ladies, and later at the ball when he bruises Sarah's arm.

A statue is something which does not usually share the brevity and vulnerability of a human life. The Majestic's Venus possesses miraculous qualities since it survives the conflagration which destroys and levels the hotel itself. This is in stark contrast to the statue of Queen Victoria, which is blown up by Republicans and mutilated. The Venus, by contrast, stands amid the ash and rubble, its whiteness unblemished, 'strangely undamaged' (p. 446). As an artefact invulnerable to the ravages of time the statue has something in common with a work of art such as a poem or a novel. It is poignant and appropriate that the hotel's statue should be of the goddess of love. Love symbolically survives amid the destruction caused by hatred and revenge. It also survives carnally (in the shape of Viola O'Neill's pregnancy) and platonically (in the form of the Major's unrequited love for Sarah). But love is also a burden: the Major is 'still troubled' (p. 446) when he leaves Ireland. It is only when he ceases to think about Sarah that he is liberated.

The underlying philosophy of the novel therefore has less to do with loving other people than with sustaining a stoic detachment in the face of the tragic condition of humanity. Dr

Ryan articulates this best when, after observing that people are only with us for a while and then they disappear (i.e. die), he adds, 'and there is nothing to be done about it. . . . A man must not let himself become bitter and defeated because of this state of affairs, because really there is no point in it' (p. 154). This is where there is a crucial difference in tone between *Troubles* and Farrell's previous books. Each of the three earlier novels conveys a harsh, absurdist view of life as empty and unredeemable. The humour of these novels glitters with cynical wit, whereas in *Troubles* there is altogether more compassion and a weary resignation about the foibles and weaknesses of mankind.

*Troubles* begins and ends by cutting down to size its central subject, the Majestic, and implicitly disclaiming any belief in its intrinsic importance. Farrell conveys a specifically post-modern sense of the arbitrary nature of formal structures and plots, including those impinged upon by the plots of history. The novel begins by revealing its ending and disposes of heroic perspectives by expressing an absurdist vision of civilization and imperial grandeur as a matter, ultimately, of basins, bathtubs and lavatory bowls. In the long perspective history is cut down to size: in the long run there is only oblivion. Novels, like statues of Venus, survive the holocaust of time, and Farrell seems to suggest that, like the Major, we must resign ourselves to such small and melancholy consolations.

# 4

## A WORLD TURNED UPSIDE DOWN

> I cannot part with the subject of India without some
> concluding remarks. The profound hypocrisy and inherent
> barbarism of bourgeois civilisation lies unveiled before our
> eyes, turning from its home, where it assumes respectable
> forms, to the colonies, where it goes naked. (Karl Marx, 'The
> Future Results of the British Rule in India')

The Indian Mutiny, which provides the setting for Farrell's
second historical novel, was 'a traumatic event . . . destroying
the myth of the grateful and obedient natives being led on-
wards and upwards by the paternal white ruler' (MD1). It
began at Meerut in northern India in May 1857 and then
spread to Delhi and other military posts. The Mutiny never
became a general uprising and the sepoys (or Indian soldiers)
were unable to organize and co-ordinate their command.
Additional British troops were despatched to India and the
rebellion was finally decisively crushed with great brutality in
1858. The Mutiny, with its disturbing revelations of Indian
insubordination, proved unforgettable, even in the modern
Raj. In *A Passage to India* (1924) McBryde sternly tells
Fielding: 'Read any of the Mutiny records; which, rather than
the Bhagavad Gita should be your Bible in this country.'[40]

*The Siege of Krishnapur* lies outside the broad tradition of
British fiction about India. It is not a 'condition of India' novel
and does not attempt centrally to address the vexed topic of
Anglo-Indian relations, as E. M. Forster did or, more recently,
Paul Scott in the 'Raj Quartet' (1966–75). Farrell's interest lies
less in the causes of the Mutiny or its historical developments
than in the condition of an isolated community caught up in the
dramatic experience of being besieged. He based his narrative

largely on histories and memoirs of the Siege of Lucknow but transferred the action of his novel to a fictitious settlement, Krishnapur (which means 'city of Krishna'). This allowed Farrell to use history in a very flexible way. During the Siege of Lucknow loyal Indians left the city and passed through the sepoy lines with messages for Brigadier Havelock, who was leading a relief column. Nothing like this occurs in *The Siege of Krishnapur*, since Farrell is interested in emphasizing the utter isolation of his embattled community. Farrell also omits some of the messier historical anomalies, such as the discovery, made by a member of the force which relieved Lucknow, of a massive cache of supplies concealed beneath the Residency building. These supplies had been stored there by Sir Henry Lawrence, the Chief Commissioner for Oudh, who died before telling anyone of their existence.

*The Siege of Krishnapur* is a kind of pastiche Victorian novel, written from an ironic twentieth-century perspective. As such it has certain similarities with John Fowles's *The French Lieutenant's Woman* (1969). Both novelists draw on the conventions of popular fiction in order to recreate a vanished era and both use parody and pastiche to establish the ironic distance between nineteenth- and twentieth-century perceptions of both history and narrative. There the resemblances largely end. Farrell synthesized his novel from a mass of Victorian documents and examines a major moment of nineteenth-century history, whereas *The French Lieutenant's Woman* is largely set in a rural backwater and is more centrally concerned with the theme of individual authenticity. The two novels are also set in crucially different years: in 1857 Darwin's *Origin of Species* had not yet been published and Victorian self-confidence was at its height. Ten years later (when Fowles's novel is set) other forces, both intellectual and political, were stirring.

Farrell explained that he deliberately set *The Siege of Krishnapur* in a period when 'the Empire was at its most energetic thanks to the new technology of the Industrial Revolution and seemed to be offering (in many ways it was offering) a vast range of physical, social and moral benefits' (MD1). Farrell conjures up the Victorian middle-class mood of optimism and benign complacency in the first five chapters of the novel, and personifies it in the figure of Mr Hopkins, 'the Collector' (of taxes) and senior administrator of the region. The Collector speaks eloquently of the spreading of the Gospel on the one hand and of the spreading of the railways on the other:

> I believe that we are all part of a society which by its communal efforts of faith and reason is gradually raising itself to a higher state. . . . Mrs Lang, we are raising ourselves, however painfully, so that mankind may enjoy in the future a superior life which now we can hardly conceive! The foundations on which the new men will build their lives are Faith, Science, Respectability, Geology, Mechanical Invention, Ventilation and Rotation of Crops! (*SK*, p. 80)

The greatest event in the Collector's life has been his attendance at the Great Exhibition held in Hyde Park in 1851. There the goods of 14,000 exhibitors were on display, representing Victorian commerce at its most buoyant. The Collector (whose official title carries an ironic metaphorical meaning) has cluttered the Residency with objects from the Exhibition which he has proudly brought over to India. These objects, many of which will seem bizarre, tasteless or comically preposterous to modern eyes, are regarded by Mr Hopkins as the concrete embodiment of a progressive and rational civilization.

Not everyone shares the Collector's enthusiasm. Fleury, a romantic young dilettante who is over in India on a visit, remarks that 'the Great Exhibition was not, as everyone said it was, a landmark of civilization; it was for the most part a collection of irrelevant rubbish' (p. 82). But Fleury, as his name suggests, is a hopelessly impractical and rather flowery young man (he even writes 'in a flowery hand' (p. 37)), whose daydreaming almost brings about his death. A more cogent critique of the Exhibition is made by the Magistrate, a man 'impermeable to optimism where social improvements were concerned' (p. 123). When the Collector praises Prince

Albert's Model Houses for the Labouring Classes the Magistrate cynically retorts that what prompted such 'trivial improvements' (p. 124) was the fear of a cholera epidemic among the wealthier classes.

Later, as the Mutiny erupts and the siege begins, references to the Great Exhibition form an increasingly ironic counter-point to the shocking realities which the defenders find them-selves having to face up to. In the first five chapters, however, Farrell lets the complacencies of Victorian India show them-selves in small ways. Harry Dunstaple's knowledge of the Indian language is, we learn, 'limited to a few simple com-mands, domestic and military' (p. 43). Miriam is given a tour of the opium factory outside Krishnapur and neither she nor anyone else in the English expatriate community finds this trade at all incongruous (although in fact there was a century-long campaign in Britain against the opium trade). In the second chapter the topic of mutinous sepoys and potential problems over the introduction of the new cartridges is broached for the first time. The news of trouble at Barrackpur and Berhampur is blithely dismissed: 'But there was no cause for alarm and, besides, now that everyone had finished eating, a game of blind man's buff was being called for' (p. 32). The game provides an apt visual symbol of the blindness expressed at the beginning of the sentence, since there is in reality every cause for alarm regarding the threatening situation then de-veloping in northern India. Farrell neatly links one kind of complacency with another sort by his emphasis on the full stomachs of his English characters. Food and eating are central subjects in *The Siege of Krishnapur*: from the lavish picnic in the Botanical Gardens, with its ham, oysters, pickles, cheese, tongue, chickens, chocolate and other delicacies, the narrative moves on to Krishnapur and a sumptuous dinner at the Resi-dency, with fried fish, curried fowl and roast kid, followed by a creamy mango fool. The gluttony of these well-fed colonists is destined shortly to give way to the privations of a siege, and within a relatively short time they are reduced to eating almost anything at all.

There is one other way in which Farrell prepares the reader for the shocking surprises which are in store for the expatriate community of Krishnapur. This is by his emphasis on the isolation of the city amid the vastness of the Indian sub-continent (one need only look at a map of India and examine the position of Lucknow, on which Farrell based Krishnapur, to understand something of this). Krishnapur is only tenuously linked to Calcutta and the coast by a carriage that brings mail and occasional visitors once a fortnight across 'the vast plain' (p. 41). The isolation of Krishnapur has parallels with that of Kurtz's Inner Station in *Heart of Darkness*. Farrell's India, like Conrad's Africa, is portrayed as a vast, incomprehensible land that makes the pretensions of the white man seem puny and absurd. When the Collector bellows 'about the progress of mankind, about the ventilation of populous quarters of cities, about the conquest of ignorance and prejudice by the glistening sabre of men's intelligence' (p. 80) Farrell adds the telling detail that 'the Collector's shouts rang emptily over the Indian plain which stretched for hundreds of miles in every direction' (p. 81). The image of 'the vast and empty plain' is repeated throughout the novel. The Collector's monologue on progress is echoed in the scene where the Padre walks around the defences of the besieged city shouting to the Lord: once again the voice of a white man is lost 'in the vast silence of the Indian plain' (p. 133).

Farrell also imitates the well-known scene in *Heart of Darkness* in which the futility and near-insanity of colonialism is summed up by the sight of a man-of-war shelling the bush; during the siege Fleury fires off a cannon and sends 'a black ball sailing towards the dark rim of melon beds, into which it presently vanished with no visible effect whatsoever' (p. 136). Farrell's India, like Conrad's Africa, is opaque and im-penetrable, a continent of alien languages and religions, its people mysterious, its signs impossible to decode through a white man's eyes. Each night of the siege the Collector is perplexed by the sight of mysterious fires burning around the enclave:

Were they signals? Nobody knew. But every night they reappeared. Other, more distant bonfires could be seen from the roof, burning mysteriously by themselves out there on the empty plain where in normal times there was nothing but darkness. (p. 174)

Neither the Collector nor the reader ever learns the meaning of these fires.

In the early chapters, by contrast, India seems familiar and domesticated. The Collector gazes at his Residency with satisfaction, reflecting that 'it was hard to believe that one was in India at all, except for the punkahs' (p. 16); the splendid scene at the ball in Calcutta makes it seem 'as if all this were taking place not in India but in some temperate land far away' (p. 41). The Mutiny shatters these illusions and shows how thinly the layer of 'English civilization' lies upon India. The forms of English life appear absurd in an Indian context. The Maharajah's Prime Minister, for example, is an utterly inscrutable figure:

Looking at the Prime Minister the Collector was overcome by a feeling of helplessness. He realized that there was a whole way of life of the people in India which he would never get to know and which was totally indifferent to him and his concerns. (p. 210)

As the siege wears on, India reverts to its true identity, and the plain becomes 'that vast, *hostile* plain' (p. 245, my italics).

*

In *The Siege of Krishnapur* Farrell develops his interest in the theme of illness and disease. As in *Troubles* sickness functions as a metaphor for the rottenness of the imperial order. The Joint Magistrate is absent from Krishnapur, having 'gone to the hills for a cure from which it was feared he would not return' (p. 42). The Collector's wife is in poor health and is despatched home to England; her youngest child has died of ill-health only six months earlier. Dr McNab's wife has died from cholera. Mr Donnelly dies of a heart attack and so, too, does Dr Dunstaple. During the course of the siege Mrs Scott gives birth but the baby is stillborn and she herself expires shortly afterwards. In August two more babies are born and one dies almost immediately. Little Mary Porter dies. This inventory of sickness and death is in a sense more credible and realistic than that found in *Troubles*, since India in the nineteenth century was a land with a high mortality rate amongst Europeans.

Farrell treats the theme of the body and sickness realistically in three ways. Firstly, the privations of the siege shred the dignity and prudery of the female characters. Louise suffers from a red spot on her forehead and a boil on her neck but takes some comfort from the fact that she smells less than many of the other ladies. Earlier, Fleury has noted the terrible effects of the Indian climate on English women: 'The flesh subsides and melts away, leaving only strings and fibres and wrinkles' (p. 39). By the end of the siege the last vestiges of Louise's snobbery have been stripped away by the naked need to survive.

Secondly, the weakness and vulnerability of the body comically undermines the high-flown intellectual debates between the leading protagonists. Fleury sums this up when he morosely reflects that 'the higher his spirit soared, the more his face, neck and armpits seeped ... but such is man's estate' (p. 118). Lastly, Farrell shows a great interest in medical debate as an expression of the battle between tradition and orthodoxy on the one hand, and rationality and innovation on the other. The real hero of the novel is Dr McNab, who has all the features of the classic Farrell protagonist: 'His manner was formal and reticent; although still quite young he had a middle-aged and melancholy air and, like many gloomy people, he looked discreet' (p. 60). McNab is a quiet, unassuming man committed to detached observation (even of his dying wife – to the outrage of the pompous and traditional Dr Dunstaple) and the empirical investigation of disease. The clash between the two doctors regarding the cause and proper treatment of cholera is a paradigm of the battle between the best and worst elements of the Victorian mind. As the Collector finally acknowledges, McNab was 'The only one who knew what he was doing' (p. 312).

Although the theme of illness received a much broader naturalistic treatment in *The Siege of Krishnapur* than in *Troubles* its metaphorical implications are inescapable. Dr Dunstaple complacently describes western civilization as 'A beneficial disease' (p. 38) but the metaphor soon rebounds upon the standard bearers of Empire. The ominous distribution of chapatis described in the first chapter sweeps the countryside 'like an epidemic' (p. 10), and when the siege is finally over the giant busts of Plato and Socrates survive, but 'terribly pocked by round shot and musket fire, as if by a disfiguring disease' (p. 308). The description of the Residency surrounded by fire 'like some mysterious sign isolating a contagion from the dark countryside' (p. 127) alludes to the Oran of Camus's *The Plague* (1947). In Camus's novel the plague is a metaphor for fascism, a terrible invading force infecting a city's population. Camus laconically describes how even in death 'the authorities still gave thought to propriety'[41] by reserving one pit for the corpses of men, the other for women. This is echoed by Farrell in the blackly comic scene in which Father O'Hara, the Padre and the Collector quarrel over which one of three shrouded bodies is the Catholic corpse. The cholera outbreak which erupts within the besieged encampment of Krishnapur is, like Camus's plague, a manifestation of moral decay and sickness. Even the Collector falls ill (though of erysipelas rather than cholera) and becomes delirious. His recovery coincides with the abandonment of his social idealism: in a sense he recovers from the disease of civilization. Some of the other Europeans are not so fortunate. The cases of 'partial blindness' and 'swollen heads' (p. 279) which affect the community seem like a physiological manifestation of their moral myopia.

*

When he was asked why he had chosen the Indian Mutiny as a subject, Farrell explained that he wanted to write 'a novel of ideas which could be read at the same time simply as an adventure story . . . adventure was what the Victorians most loved after profits and respectability' (MD1). As an adventure story *The Siege of Krishnapur* relies for its suspense on the question of whether or not the besieged community will succeed in holding off the sepoys until help comes. In fact the experience of siege becomes almost a permanent condition, and Farrell plays down the chronology of events. The siege lasts three and a half months, from June until mid-September 1857, but Farrell is less interested in the historical development of the Mutiny than in the effects of siege on his central characters.

In the foreground of the novel are the Collector, Fleury, the Magistrate and the Padre, who all hold strong opinions about human nature. The Padre represents Christian dogmatism in the period immediately prior to publication of *The Origin of Species* in 1859. He is an adherent of the argument that the existence of God can be proved by the evidence of design in the universe. When Fleury ventures a mild criticism of this rather geometrical theology it results in the Padre becoming comically obsessed by the notion that the sepoy Mutiny is God's punishment for the presence of a dangerous freethinker like Fleury in their midst. The Padre is completely unchanged by the siege, other than in transferring his righteous anger to what he perceives as the idolatry of the Crystal Palace. For Fleury, however, the siege comes as 'a solstice' (p. 187) in his life: 'He grew steadily less responsive to beauty and steadily more bluff, good-natured and interested in physical things' (p. 187). Fleury is a dilettante who has it in him to become a great creative, inventive figure, but who settles in the end for marriage, hedonism and the straitjacket of intellectual orthodoxy.

The Magistrate, by contrast, is a sceptic and his criticisms of imperial rule make his the most modern voice in the novel. However, the Magistrate's scepticism is corroded by his cynicism. In abandoning any belief in the possibility of changing the selfishness of men or the corruption of imperial India the Magistrate finds intellectual refuge in the deterministic pseudo-science of phrenology.

Lastly there is the Collector with his enormous faith in a beneficial and superior civilization. The Collector's idealism is immune to the cynical sniping of the Magistrate, but is gradually worn down by the siege. Loss of faith in civilization is followed by the loss of his religious faith as 'the foxes of despair . . . continued to raid his beliefs' (pp. 234–5).

Farrell's narrative technique is mock-Victorian: leisurely, omniscient and authoritative. He imitates the confident Victorian tone of voice but the authority of the narrative is invariably informed by irony. We are told that the Maharajah of Krishnapur 'did not want Progress . . . he wanted money, jewels and naked girls, or rather, since he already had all of these things, he wanted more of them' – to which the narrator adds, 'Hari, like any reasonable person, found these desires (money, jewels, naked girls) incomprehensible' (p. 126). The relaxed, intimate tone in which the narrator addresses the reader sometimes gives way disconcertingly – as in the comically shocking impropriety of the sentence which begins, 'If you had lifted the dresses of the Krishnapur ladies on that morning of the last assault' (p. 286).

As well as gently mocking the authority of Victorian narrative Farrell self-consciously recreates through parody and pastiche a narrative reverberating with echoes of Victorian and other writers, heightening the sense of grotesquerie and irony as a range of half-familiar literary characters are exposed to a brutal, extreme, tragic situation. The scene in the Dunstaple household when Fleury and Miriam first arrive is a pastiche of all those scenes in Jane Austen where the ladies furtively stare from an upper window at a visiting eligible bachelor. While the Mutiny rages beyond the ramparts a more traditional sort of warfare is going on within, for, as Louise puts it, 'to have their hearts besieged and captured' (p. 191) is one of the things that men are here for. Lucy, Louise and Miriam are in fact very reminiscent of Jane Austen characters and like them can be ranked on a scale involving gradations of self-delusion. Lucy and Louise are both, in a modest fashion, snobs and poseurs, but each gets the man she deserves. Miriam's dryly ironic manner and quiet detachment put her rather higher on the scale than the other two and it comes as no surprise to learn that she eventually marries Dr McNab.

Fleury is known to his sister Miriam as 'Dobbin', and both his clumsiness and his name recall the Dobbin in Thackeray's *Vanity Fair* (1848). Thackeray's father was a Collector in Bengal and his Dobbin, like Fleury, plans to complete a book about India. Another character in *The Siege of Krishnapur* who seems in part to derive from *Vanity Fair* is Lucy, whose melting vulnerability and beauty is reminiscent of Amelia Sedley. But Fleury also owes something to Fabrizio in Stendhal's *The Charterhouse of Parma* (1839). Fabrizio is a melancholy romantic, perpetually agitated by 'feelings', who frequently finds himself involved in absurd, comic misadventures. His absent-minded daydreaming in the middle of the Battle of Waterloo and his sense of self-satisfaction at becoming 'a real soldier'[42] are duplicated by Fleury's comical daydreams during the first sepoy attack. Fabrizio's misadventures with a 'huge, straight, heavy cavalry sword, which was much too ponderous for him'[43] seem to have inspired Fleury's near-disastrous experiment with the Fleury Cavalry Eradicator. Finally, Fabrizio's terrifying battle with Giletti is imitated in the scene where Fleury battles with a burly sepoy.

Vokins, on the other hand, seems to have come straight out of Dickens, and some critics have also detected parallels between Farrell's Indian fiction and the novels of Mrs Gaskell, Trollope and P. G. Wodehouse.[44] A more explicit literary borrowing occurs in chapter 19 where the Collector, feverish from erysipelas, watched the sepoys launch a major attack. It is 'a scene which reminded the Collector of the beach':

How pleasant it is to sit on the cliffs of Dover and watch the waves rolling in. You can see them beginning so far out . . . you see them slowly grow as they come nearer and nearer to the shore, rise and then thrash themselves against the beach. Some of them vanish inexplicably. Others turn themselves into giants. As the sepoys, sensing that their chance had now come to abolish the *feringhees* from the face of the earth, massed for a great assault, the Collector could see that a giant wave was coming. (pp. 215–16)

This passage involves an unmistakable allusion to Matthew Arnold's 'Dover Beach', commonly regarded as his finest poem and distinguished by an almost modern sense of *Angst* and doubt. The 'giant wave' of mutinous sepoys attacking the besieged encampment is destined to rob the Collector of both his religious faith and his faith in progress, echoing the devastating global retreat of the 'Sea of Faith' described in Arnold's poem. 'Dover Beach' was first published in 1867, ten years after the Mutiny and eight years after *The Origin of Species* first appeared, and its concluding lines, though metaphorical, have an ironically literal application to the situation of the Europeans besieged at Krishnapur, whose world also

> Hath really neither joy, nor love, nor light,
> Nor certitude, nor peace, nor help for pain;
> And we are here as on a darkling plain
> Swept with confused alarms of struggle and flight,
> Where ignorant armies clash by night.

Alone of the characters in *The Siege of Krishnapur* the Collector is emotionally maimed by the experience of siege, and returns to England in a mood of deep depression and disillusion. By the end of the book his idealism and optimism are blasted and his mood is every bit as dejected and perturbed as that of the speaker in 'Dover Beach'. Perhaps it is no coincidence that the Collector shares the same surname as that of another Victorian poet, G. M. Hopkins, whose so-called 'terrible sonnets' also explore a nightmare world of spiritual disillusion, doubt and anxiety. The Collector's sensitivity to the ugly truths exposed at Krishnapur is in stark contrast to the complacency of the other characters, especially Fleury. Fleury sheds his romantic sensitivity and his sceptical, critical attitude to colonial life and comes through unscathed. Although he has the potential to anticipate not only the theory of evolution but also the invention of motion film Fleury turns instead into a stout, opinionated, utterly conventional (and hypocritical) Victorian gentleman.

What this web of literary echoings and allusions indicates is the richness and variety of Farrell's stylistic synthesis. The narrative shifts unobtrusively from a kind of neutral realism into black and sometimes surrealistic farce and back again. The elasticity of Farrell's narrative tone is indicated by his presentation of the hideous pariah dog. Its loathsome appearance is described in some detail but thereafter it develops a romantic affection for Fleury and becomes a faintly comic object. Beneath the comedy, however, lies horror:

> Its mouth was open, its lips drawn back, and it appeared to be grinning. From the thin, wretched creature it had been at the beginning of the siege it had become quite fat, for recently it had succeeded in eating two small lap-dogs which had unwisely fallen asleep in its presence. . . . but most of all it would like to eat Fleury, such was the power of its love for this handsome, green-clad young man; it uttered a groan of ecstasy at the thought and a needle of saliva, dripping from its jaws, sparkled in the Collector's telescope. (pp. 213–14)

Comedy and nightmarish horror are uneasily juxtaposed in scenes like this, and there is the additional irony that the narrator's omniscience should extend to something as lowly and disgusting as a pariah dog.

Of all the texts Farrell echoes in *The Siege of Krishnapur* the one most congruent with his absurdist vision of Victorian imperialism is *Alice's Adventures in Wonderland*, first published eight years after the Mutiny, in 1865. Farrell's India is a weird, topsy-turvy land where dreams, fevers and madness are never very far away from the surface. Rayne, the Opium Agent, calls his servants by the names of animals and insects and Farrell himself frequently draws an analogy between his human characters and animals. The Collector is highly regarded by 'the "big dogs" ' (p. 17) of the East India Company, although he himself 'looked like a massive cat' (p. 26). Fleury's torpor is reminiscent of Lewis Carroll's Dormouse, and at one point it seems as if the Magistrate's 'eyes, nose and ears were floating disembodied above [his] morning coat' (p. 101), giving him a resemblance to the Cheshire Cat. The Collector's absurd, dogged insistence on playing croquet with his 'swooning elder daughters' on a 'sweltering patch of sun-baked earth' (p. 67) calls to mind Alice's vain endeavours on the Queen of Hearts's croquet-ground – as does the narrator's eccentric request to the reader to 'Picture a map of India as big as a tennis court with two or three hedgehogs crawling over it' (p. 91).

The surrealist yoking together of the real and the fantastic is sustained through the novel. Harry Dunstaple gazes rapturously at his brass cannon as if it is the body of a naked young girl; later, when he and Fleury find a real naked young girl on their hands, they are immensely puzzled by their first sight of female pubic hair and diligently attempt to scrape it off. Krishnapur is never very far from the zany logic of Alice's Wonderland (Mrs Dunstaple, for example, is 'put to bed on her shelf in the pantry' (p. 271)). The juxtaposition of wildly incongruous things – General Jackson's wounds and a slice of toast and honey (p. 89); mutinous sepoys and flies on a treacle pudding (p. 138); a mutineer and a trout in a restaurant tank (p. 269) – is a striking feature of Farrell's style. These grotesque food metaphors are ironically apt in a situation where the siege's victims regress from gluttony to starvation. It is also immensely ironic that the besieged Europeans are forced to retreat to the Residency's banqueting hall, with its connotations of feudalism and vanished feasts. The Collector, like a medieval baron, ends up sitting on an oak throne which has lost one of its four legs – a striking emblem of his vanished authority and personal instability.

The opening pages of the novel prepare the reader for the fractured, unreal scenes that are to follow. The first thing Farrell stresses about India is its capacity for *distortion*. What appears to be the town of Krishnapur in 'the heat distorted distance' (p. 9) turns out to be a desolate, ancient cemetery, one of the 'Cities of the Silent'. This illusory Krishnapur is surrounded by the true India, with its 'unending plain', 'a dreary ocean of bald earth', an 'immensity' with no 'comfort' for a white man, 'nothing that a European might recognize as a civilisation' (p. 9).

The theme of distortion, misperception and illusion is in part represented by the role played in the novel by telescopes. At the beginning we are told that the Residency has two towers. One provides a base for the Union Jack (later to crash down on the Collector); 'on the other the Collector sometimes set up a telescope when the mood took him to scrutinize the heavens' (p. 13). The Collector's interest in the sky expresses at once his idealism and his complacency. The reality of India under imperial rule lies all around him but it takes a Mutiny to shatter his myopia and restore his proper perception of things. The telescope, signifying science and progress, is before long employed in observing the sepoy lines. Soon the Collector's calm confidence in the superiority of European civilization begins to crumble: 'The Collector's hands trembled so badly that he had to rest the telescope on the shattered window sill' (p. 213). The telescope's 'scorching lens' (p. 213) provides him with a close-up vision of an India which has become a terrifying nightmare. The Collector watches from his room as the sepoys attack but can 'no longer understand' (p. 213) the scenes before his eyes. He moves the lens 'uncomprehendingly' (p. 213) across the field of battle, beginning with the sight of a man in the spasms of death and ending with the loathsome dog-eating, man-eating pariah dog. Finally the Collector's nerve breaks: '"Let us have tea on the lawn again!" shouted the Collector from the window, but no one paid any attention to him' (p. 214).

In fact a number of tea parties which are every bit as bizarre as the Mad Hatter's take place during the course of the siege. The first is given 'on the carpet of the Residency drawing-room, in the lee of a shattered grand piano' (p. 190). The second tea party takes place in equally ironic surroundings, with the guests 'all seated around a little fire in the middle of the floor of the banqueting hall not too far from the baronial fireplace' (p. 228). This tea party turns into absurdist farce as a cloud of cockchafers swarm into the room, filling the teacups and covering Lucy from head to toe. By the time of the third tea party there is no tea left to drink at all:

> Now in the banqueting hall another pleasant tea-party was taking place, even though tea itself was in such short supply that there was really only hot water to drink.
> 'Another cup, Mr Willoughby?' asked Lucy who, as hostess, was behaving impeccably. (p. 239)

The final tea party is the most bizarre of all. Fleury barters his gold cufflinks, a silver snuff-box and a pair of shoes for two lumps of sugar and buys a teaspoonful of tea for £10, then invites Louise to the banqueting hall for tea and cakes. Unfortunately 'they had dried as hard as the stone they were baked on, and had to be chipped off it with a bayonet' (p. 279).

By the end of the novel the English expatriates have metamorphosed into natives and the Indians are watching *them* through telescopes. While the whites starve and suffer from malnutrition the wealthier natives picnic on the slopes above the encampment and gaze down at the 'ragged, boil-covered skeletons' (p. 277) below through telescopes and opera glasses. The Collector, his notions of belonging to a superior civilization shattered, sits 'cross-legged in the native fashion' (p. 286), having arrived at the melancholy conclusion that of all his treasures brought to India from the Great Exhibition the only one which has turned out to be of real use is a case of pistols.

A criticism which has been levelled against *The Siege of Krishnapur* is that the book is really far too funny to convey effectively the underlying seriousness of Farrell's critique of Empire. Certainly one never feels that Farrell's amiable cast of characters – often 'characters' in the secondary sense of the noun – is seriously or reprehensibly involved in colonial exploitation or repression. Farrell's treatment of Empire is rather different from Forster's or George Orwell's since the predominantly comic tone of his narrative conjures away the problem of evil. *The Siege of Krishnapur* is really a kind of pastoral narrative, in William Empson's sense of putting the complex into the simple.[45] The Indian Mutiny was actually a much nastier and messier affair than it seems from Farrell's novel and *The Siege of Krishnapur* holds up, perhaps more so than he originally intended, a rather flattering image of English planning and organization. The defenders of Lucknow actually had little strategic sense of how to construct or defend fortified positions and when relief came the city was sacked by vengeful British troops.

Farrell's fictional siege ends with the General in charge of the relief column imagining how an artist might best memorialize the scene by leaving certain things absent or in soft focus – not least the corpses and the ragged survivors. But for all its witty and ironic self-consciousness about narrative, history and the Victorian self-image *The Siege of Krishnapur* also has its historical absences. The ugly end to the Mutiny, with massive and bloody reprisals inflicted indiscriminately upon sepoys and Indian civilians alike, is simply omitted in the chronological leap from September 1857 to the late 1870s which takes place at the end of the novel. At no point during the siege do Farrell's English characters discuss the motives of the sepoys or how they would like to punish them for their monstrous insubordination. Indeed, they do not discuss them at all, other than in relation to matters of strategy. In his critique of the treatment given to imperialism in the *New Cambridge Modern History* V. G. Kiernan has complained that

> Atrocities committed on both sides during the Indian Mutiny are only fleetingly mentioned. Imperial history altogether was a vastly more painful business than a reader would gain any inkling of from New Cambridge.[46]

In this respect *The Siege of Krishnapur* seems equally culpable. As Margaret Drabble has acknowledged, Farrell's sepoys 'are never shown as people at all, but merely as cannon fodder and comic fodder at that, and . . . their cause is given only the most frivolous explanation, seen, as it were, through British eyes' (*HS*, pp. 189–90).

The historical absences in *The Siege of Krishnapur* are to an extent redeemed by its dark final chapter which is wholly without humour. The admission of the speed with which the survivors returned 'to the civilized life they had been living before' (p. 311) is grimly ironic, and indicates their stupendous complacency. Only the Collector has his eyes opened by the terrible experience he has undergone. His sense of the vastness and the mysteriously alien nature of India is renewed on his journey to the railhead. The 'widening perspective' (p. 311) which the Collector encounters, though literally geographical, is also that of time and history. In the long view human lives, societies and Empires are, like sieges, only temporary affairs. Farrell dismisses the substance of his fiction, asserting 'what a small affair' the siege of Krishnapur has been, 'how unimportant, how devoid of significance' (p. 311). This gloomy view of the Collector's shattered domain takes us back to the beginning of the novel, with its modern-day description of a run-down and decayed Krishnapur, which has lost its nineteenth-century importance and now has 'the air of a place you might see in a melancholy dream' (p. 10).

At the very end of the novel the narrator's omniscience crumbles with the remark that it was 'hard to tell what [the Collector] was thinking' (p. 313) during his last conversation with Fleury. The Collector's old optimism has by this time shrunk to a weary apathy and a general disgust with culture. The narrator's final response to the Collector is ambivalent. The reader is told that the Collector 'undoubtedly felt, as many of us feel, that one uses up so many options, so much energy, simply in trying to find out what life is all about. And as for being able to do anything about it, well . . .' (p. 313). This suggests that quietism and resignation are the only proper responses to life.

The reference to Dr McNab, however, indicates an alternative and more positive approach to human existence. The penultimate sentence of the novel tentatively suggests that the Collector may have been thinking of two Indians drawing water from a well – a scene which sums up India for him, presumably in the way it shows lives which are functioning perfectly satisfactorily without the assistance of western culture, ideas or technology. Nevertheless, within the decaying system of Empire it is McNab, with his wry, detached empirical researches into sickness and disease, who shows the way forward.

'Perhaps,' the narrator concludes, 'by the very end of his life, in 1880, [the Collector] had come to believe that a people, a nation, does not create itself according to its own best ideas, but is shaped by other forces of which it has little knowledge' (p. 313). Exactly what some of those un-named, enigmatic 'other forces' might be was to form the subject of Farrell's last completed novel, his ambitious epic *The Singapore Grip*.

*

*The Hill Station*, which forms a kind of modest sequel to *The Siege of Krishnapur*, is set largely in Simla in 1871. It reintroduces from the earlier book the figure of Dr McNab, still living in Krishnapur with Fleury's sister Miriam. McNab is now middle-aged and struggling to complete a massively researched treatise on Indian Medicine. The Mutiny, which never reached as far as Simla, is now just a fading memory. The McNabs's niece is dimly aware that her uncle and aunt 'had met under strained circumstances . . . in some battle or other with lots of flies about and without clothes on' (*HS*, p. 92). *The Hill Station* is set in the middle of the long period of civil peace in India which lasted from the suppression of the Mutiny up until the 1890s.

The plot of *The Hill Station* centres on a doctrinal row about ritualism which has broken out in Simla between Kingston, a tubercular clergyman, and his Bishop. A parallel sub-plot follows the fortunes of Mrs Forester, an outcast from polite society because of her flagrant liaisons. The narrator's laconic observation that 'Fashion has this in common with religion: if you believe in it, it works' (p. 94) establishes the connection between religious form and the rigid rules of fashionable Simla society. Had Farrell lived to complete the novel he would presumably have amplified a range of contrasts which are set out in the opening chapters between Simla and the rest of India and within Simla itself. Simla is a domain 'up there' (p. 39), cool, fashionable and heavenly and very different from the hot, hellish, dusty India of the plains below. But Simla itself is a divided realm, both spiritually, in the clash between high and low church, and socially, in the descent from Elisium House to the Lower Bazaar. The final contrast is between the remote, high Himalayas and the insignificant squabbles of Simla's men and women.

The real thrust of *The Hill Station* would seemingly have been less concerned with either religious ritual or social satire than with a development of Farrell's interest in the theme of sickness. Once again Farrell portrays a world where sickness is omnipresent. McNab's niece, Emily, has a paralysed hand, the hotel owner Mr Lowrie suffers from a heart condition, Mr Forsythe, the curate, is sick with fever, and one of the young curates at Elysium House has a swollen gland in his neck. The chief focus of interest is Mr Kingston, who displays all the symptoms of suffering from tuberculosis, a subject Farrell clearly intended to explore with the same relish for encyclopaedic detail that he brought to cholera in *The Siege of Krishnapur*. *The Hill Station* would apparently have taken Farrell's interest in sickness a stage further by exploring some of its psychological and spiritual dimensions, illustrated in the clash between Mr Kingston and the Bishop. Both men are sick and both are able to transcend physical incapacity by sheer force of will. Farrell's notes for the unwritten part of the novel suggest that Kingston would have resigned from the Church at the request of the apparently dying Bishop, leave Simla and die. A note by Farrell indicates the mordant and melancholy conclusion which the book would have had: 'The Bishop, recovered, is playing croquet again. Another curate-challenger. McNab does not wait, he knows how it will end' (p. 175).

*The Hill Station* would evidently have been Farrell's homage to one of his favourite novels, Thomas Mann's *The Magic Mountain* (1924), a book which also considers how a man at odds with his times may suffer 'a certain laming of the personality . . . a sort of palsy, as it were, which may even extend from his spiritual and moral over into his physical and organic part'.[47] *The Magic Mountain* portrays a sick community on the brink of the apocalypse of the First World War. Farrell's Simla is not under such an immediate threat of annihilation but the reader is nevertheless permitted a glimpse of its eventual demise:

> as Emily, light as a feather, went bobbing away on the strong brown shoulders of her *jampanis*, a few thousand miles away in London a familiar bearded leonine figure sucking a pencil turned a little in his seat in the British Museum to see the hands of the clock at the northern quarter of the Reading Room, and thought, 'Soon it will be closing time.' (p. 92)

The figure is, of course, Karl Marx. The first volume of *Capital* had been published four years earlier, in 1867, and did indeed spell 'closing time' for Emily's world of privileged supremacy. The economic basis of imperialism, scarcely touched on in *Troubles* or *The Siege of Krishnapur*, forms the central theme of Farrell's last completed work, *The Singapore Grip*.

# 5

## APOCALYPSE

> Politics, in a literary work, are like a pistol-shot in the middle of a concert, something loud and out of place, yet something all the same to which we cannot refuse to pay attention.
> (Stendhal, *The Charterhouse of Parma*)

Farrell's ironic vision of imperial decline reached its apotheosis with *The Singapore Grip*, unquestionably his *magnum opus*, a massively conceived novel set in the weeks and days prior to the surrender of Singapore to Japanese troops during the Second World War. *The Singapore Grip* was, in the words of one reviewer 'planned on a scale as grand as Tolstoy's [*War and Peace*]'[48] but equally it can be set alongside other ambitious attempts to fictionalize some of the epic yet blackly farcical episodes of the 1939–45 war, ranging from Thomas Pynchon's *Gravity's Rainbow* (1973) to J. G. Ballard's *Empire of the Sun* (1983). The fall of Singapore in 1942 provided Farrell with an appropriately apocalyptic terminus to his trilogy; its loss has been described by one historian as 'the worst single military defeat the British Empire ever suffered'.[49]

Singapore nowadays is of relatively little importance to Britain, but between 1918 and 1939 this island city was regarded as one of the jewels of the Empire. It was the major business centre of South East Asia and it dominated the maritime approaches to India, New Zealand and Australia: 'in British imperial mystique it ranked second only to the Suez Canal itself'.[50] During these years successive governments financed an immensely expensive fortification programme which was intended to make Singapore impregnable to assault, the so-called 'Gibraltar of the Far East'. 'Fortress Singapore' became a legendary component of British imperial supremacy and it therefore came as a shockingly unexpected and demoralizing surprise when, on 15 February 1942, the city, with a garrison of 85,000 British troops, ignominiously surrendered to a numerically-inferior invading Japanese force. Winston Churchill's comment that the loss of Singapore was 'the worst disaster and largest capitulation in British history' is often quoted. What is less well known is that as late as 10 September 1940 Churchill himself wrote:

> The probabilities of the Japanese undertaking an attack on Singapore, which would involve so large a proportion of their Fleet far outside the Yellow Sea are remote; in fact, nothing can be more foolish from their point of view.[51]

The British Prime Minister's own disingenuous and contradictory attitudes to the defence of Singapore were symptomatic of the muddle and confusion which led to the city's humiliating surrender. Probably the most glaring error on the British side was single-mindedly to gear Singapore's defences to attack from the sea, overlooking the possibility of a land-based invasion from the rear. Just as Tolstoy used real historical accounts of the Battle of Austerlitz and real historical characters like General Kutuzov, so, too, the richly documented bungling and lack of imagination on the British side furnished Farrell with a mass of factual material suitable for underpinning his fundamentally absurdist vision of recent history.

War to Farrell, as it was to Stendhal and Tolstoy, is chaotic, unheroic and often farcical. Farrell portrays Singapore as an unheroic battleground, 'drab and dismal . . . [a] grey-green slab of land surrounded by glaring water' (SG, p. 457). He delights in highlighting moments like the one where Wavell, the Supreme Commander, impatiently opens the door of his parked car at night and, not realizing that he is at the edge of the sea wall, promptly falls several feet on to some rocks. Wavell's glass eye and the all-encompassing darkness are emblematic of a much wider failure of perception and lack of clear-seeing, and Wavell's literal fall painfully anticipates the imminent 'fall' of Singapore itself. Farrell's climactic vision of 'two hostile armies

. . . struggling to subdue each other in the darkness' (p. 536) again evokes the closing lines of Arnold's 'Dover Beach'. The 'confused alarms of struggle and flight/Where ignorant armies clash by night' are re-enacted on a massive scale in *The Singapore Grip* and with an altogether darker conclusion than in *The Siege of Krishnapur*.

*The Singapore Grip* is set largely in a three-month period from mid-November 1941 to mid-February 1942, prefaced by eleven short chapters (2–12) which serve to introduce the Blackett family and which are set between 1937 and the summer of 1941. The Blacketts are among the least sympathetic characters Farrell created in any of his novels. Walter Blackett is a manipulative, vastly successful capitalist, cold-bloodedly determined to marry off his daughter Joan to the best advantage of his business. Joan herself is equally devious and calculating, while her brother Monty is little more than a shallow, self-centred playboy. The human comedy in the novel originates in Walter's much-frustrated schemes for a marriage between Matthew Webb, the son of his deceased partner, and Joan. Matthew, to everyone's surprise, turns out to be possessed of a social conscience and to hold disconcertingly subversive, utopian views about human solidarity and fraternity. While the protracted and strained relationship between Joan and Matthew fails to crystallize into anything meaningful a secondary area of comedy unfolds, centred around Blackett and Webb's plans for a grand fiftieth-anniversary parade.

The rise of Blackett and Webb parallels the growth of Singapore from a small settlement into the greatest trading port of the Far East. *The Singapore Grip* is, in part, a history of Blackett and Webb, a kind of satirical equivalent of Fleury's plans in *The Siege of Krishnapur* for a book describing the beneficial and civilizing influence of the East India Company on Indian life. The name 'Blackett and Webb' is redolent of the true face of colonial enterprise, since the firm has the native rubber producers enmeshed in a spider-like web of control and exploitation and ruthlessly 'blacks' native produce to its own commercial advantage. The true harvest of such endeavour,

Farrell intimates, is smoke and ashes. At the climax of the novel 'A huge mushroom of black smoke' rises 'on a fat, black stalk':

> Soon it would cover most of the city and, indeed, of the Island itself, snowing as it came a light precipitation of oily black smuts, which clung to everything, blackening skin and clothing alike. . . . It was not long before one or two black spots of soot began to appear on Walter's white linen suit. He tried to brush them off, but that only made them worse. Soon his suit, his shirt and his face were covered in oily black smudges. (SG, pp. 507–8)

In an aptly Bunyanesque manner the moral corruption of Walter Blackett is signalled by the way in which, surrounded by hellish fires, he himself turns black, his white suit irretrievably soiled.

From the opening page of the novel Farrell underlines the fact that Singapore is built upon ambiguous and ominously symbolic terrain. We are told that when Raffles first arrived on the island it was 'largely deserted except for a prodigious quantity of rats and centipedes' (p. 9) together with some human skulls and bones. These sinister details are reminiscent of the skeletons and the 'simply prodigious number of basins and lavatory bowls' (T, p. 10) which litter the ruins of the Majestic hotel in Troubles. After purchasing the island from a native Raffles sets up a preposterous 36-foot flagpole (symbol of an overweening imperialism) and gazes up at the flag 'with rats and centipedes seething and tumbling over his shoes' (SG, p. 9). Some of the central themes of the novel are subliminally present in these opening two paragraphs, and nineteenth-century Singapore, with its legalized theft, exploitation of the native population, piracy, vermin and human waste, is an ironic miniature of its twentieth-century self. The sophisticated and prosperous colonial society which the Blacketts inhabit, though technologically advanced, is unable to free itself from the pervasive stench of moral corruption:

Old Singapore hands like Walter were used to unpleasant smells: they came from everywhere . . . from the drains and from the river above all, but also from less likely places, from Tanglin rose-gardens for instance, where the 'boys' some-times failed to bury properly the household excrement, or someone's spaniel dug it up again. In Singapore you could never be quite safe: even while you stood smiling fixedly under the great candelabra in the ballroom at Government House, once a gift from the Emperor Franz Josef to the third Duke of Buckingham, you might suddenly get a distinct whiff of something disagreeable. (p. 506)

What is striking about the novel is the way in which Farrell uses the form of the popular 'blockbuster' to convey what is at heart a bitterly ironic and politically highly-charged vision of Empire. *The Singapore Grip* is Farrell's most obviously access-ible and cinematic novel, offering an exotic location, romance and dramatic wartime events. One reviewer's enthusiastic description of it as 'an exciting adventure story, with powerful descriptions of air-raids, fires on the docks and fighting in the jungle'[52] was amplified by the *Book of the Month Club* maga-zine, which enticed its readers with a thrilling description of the way the novel unravelled Singapore's mysteries, 'from the rich and starchy European clubs to sleazy Indian brothels. . . . Amid bombings, terrible fires and general panic, Matthew and a beautiful Eurasian girl try to escape. . . . This is a long, satisfying adventure story of a high order, wonderfully entertaining.'[53]

The blockbuster is a type of corrupt romance form of the nineteenth-century historical novel, and *The Singapore Grip* ironically and self-consciously occupies a position somewhere between the two genres. Farrell certainly seems to have in-tended the reader to have *War and Peace* in mind when reading *The Singapore Grip*. As a number of reviewers noted, Matthew Webb appears to be consciously modelled on Tolstoy's Pierre Bezuhov. The protracted death of old Mr Webb echoes that of Count Bezuhov. The deathbed scene in which the dying Count makes unintelligible requests is duplicated in *The Singapore Grip* in those scenes where Mr Webb calls out for his son, only to be misunderstood by those around him, who think he is referring, incomprehensibly, to the sun or to the political leader Sun Yat-sen. It is perhaps also significant that *War and Peace* begins with Anna Pavlovna 'suffering from an attack of *la grippe* – *grippe* being then a new word only used by a few people'.[54] When Matthew asks Dupigny what the Singapore 'grip' is the Frenchman mistakenly assumes that the expression derives from *la grippe* (the French word for influenza) and explains that it means 'a certain tropical fever, very grave' (*SG*, p. 146). The metaphorical significance of the term only emerges in its full force later, when it becomes apparent that the doom of Singapore and its people results from 'the grip of the self-interested and corrupt on human affairs' (p. 498). Like *War and Peace*, Farrell's novel has an epic breadth and fictionalizes scenes from both the highest and lowest quarters of society. *The Singapore Grip* also marks a new development in Farrell's *oeuvre* in that it gets inside the minds of both the victims of colonialism (the wharf-coolie, the inmates of the Chinese dying-house) and of the Japanese invaders. No longer is the collapse of Empire seen exclusively from the perspective of the colonial élite.

But equally Farrell's novel exploits the conventions and form of the blockbuster, often with a satirical intent. As Max Hastings noted, in *The Singapore Grip* Farrell does things with the historical novel 'that G. A. Henty and Georgette Heyer never dreamed of. His characters revel in their own mediocrity. Far from cultivating suspense, he sends them marching to their fate with the wry resignation of a professional executioner.'[55] One of the funniest moments in the novel occurs when, in a crisp parody of the stereotyped conventions of a Mills and Boon romance, Farrell reveals the nature of Vera Chiang's lust for Matthew:

'How attractive he is!' Vera was thinking. 'How stooping and shortsighted! What deliciously round shoulders and unhealthy complexion!' She gazed at him in wonder, reflecting that there was no way in which he could be improved. Indeed, she could hardly keep her eyes off him. For the fact was that Vera had been brought up, as Chinese girls had been for centuries, to find stooping, bespectacled, scholarly-looking young men attractive. (p. 340)

In Farrell's fiction human beings rarely live up to conventional expectation. Even Sir Thomas Raffles, the great imperialist, turns out to be 'by no means the lantern-jawed individual you might have expected: indeed, a rather vague-looking man in a frock coat' (p. 9). The Major puts in a welcome reappearance from *Troubles* and once more fails to live up to his dashing martial rank, representing again a kind of old-fashioned liberal decency which is hopelessly out of its depth in an absurd modern world. This is underlined by the episode parodying the churchyard scene in *Hamlet* (V.i), with the Major incongruously occupying the role of the Prince:

'Ah, Cheong,' said the Major peering into the grave where, however, nothing could be seen but the well-polished toes of a pair of stout English shoes. 'Good show,' he added, wanting to make it clear how much he appreciated Cheong's efforts.

'Whose grave is that?'

Cheong, without pausing in his digging, muttered a name which the Major had to cup his ear to catch.

'Not old Tom Prescott!' cried the Major in dismay. 'Why, François, I knew him well. He used to do a trick at parties with an egg.' And the Major gazed into the grave with concern.

. . . 'Poor old Tommy,' he said. 'What a card he was! He used to have us in fits. Mind you, he was getting on in years. He'd had a good innings.' (pp. 462–3)

This scene illustrates the manner in which the language of Farrell's characters often seems inadequate to the melancholy or nightmarish reality they are trying to come to terms with or to communicate. They frequently speak or think in tired middle-class clichés which serve to highlight the way in which these colonialists are out of touch with the strange, unfamiliar terrain in which they find themselves. Just beyond the cosy suburb of Tanglin where the Blacketts and the other affluent whites live there lies the jungle, a domain equally as alien and terrifying as the jungle in *Heart of Darkness*. Charlie Blackett (the only member of the family possessed of any sensitivity or finer feelings) is oppressed by the jungle's silence:

> There was something about this silence. . . . During the daytime when you stopped moving everything stopped, as if you were on the floor of a dead ocean. Everything had to come from *you*, that was what was so intolerable. (pp. 367–8)

Ultimately Charlie is 'swallowed up' (p. 381) by the jungle and vanishes, never to be seen again.

Tanglin itself is a suburb under threat, 'ready to burst at the seams with a dreadful tropical energy' (p. 11), waiting to be recaptured by nature. As usual in Farrell reality is all a question of perspective. Singapore is an island where 'it was hard to see any distance, except upwards' (p. 423). Self-interest and upward mobility are the keynotes of colonial life, and Walter worries that a change of environment may damage 'the sensible perspective' (p. 421) which his ruthlessly egocentric daughter has acquired in Singapore. Malaya, we are told, is a region where the eye, as a rule, cannot see very far. Nevertheless *The Singapore Grip* contains two grim scenes (the destruction of the elderly Chinese wharf-coolie in chapter 27 and the huge mushroom of black smoke in chapter 64) which look forward in time to the atom bomb attack on Hiroshima. The novel darkly intimates that at some time in the future Singapore will revert to what it was when Raffles first arrived – namely, a deserted island where 'people had once lived' (p. 9), covered in human remains, rats and centipedes.

Tanglin and the rest of European Singapore in a sense represent the world of consciousness and the ego, while the jungle expresses the dark destructive energies of the id. This line of division also works politically, since the jungle is where much of the native population lives and is the terrain from which the invading Japanese emerge to destroy white colonial society. Social hierarchy is also graphically expressed in Joan's account of her sea voyage from Shanghai with the whites occupying the top decks, enjoying 'lovely dances and games . . . and simply enormous meals' (p. 30), while the natives are crammed into dark, stuffy, third-class dormitories in the hold below.

This division is further expressed by the way in which the naturalistic dimensions of the narrative frequently melt into farce and fantasy. As Isabel Quigly noted, Farrell's Singapore has 'a strangely dreamlike air'.[56] Surface realism frequently dissolves into fantastic episodes of comedy (naked Vera and the orang-utang) or black farce (the bungled firing of Miss Olive Kennedy-Walsh, BA (Pass Arts), H Dip Ed, TCD from a cannon at a paper armoured car). *The Singapore Grip* is a great city novel, diagnosing the condition of Singapore with an encyclopaedic breadth reminiscent of Joyce's treatment of Dublin in *Ulysses* (1922), Andrei Bely's *Petersburg* (1916) and G. Cabrera Infante's fantastic vision of Havana in *Three Trapped Tigers* (1964). As with these other city novels, the realism of *The Singapore Grip* often shades off into an hallucinatory sub-world of fantasy and parody. In fact Farrell's *magnum opus* is a curious amalgam of hard documentary detail and fiction: Singapore itself, we are reminded, is almost fictional in its origins – 'It was simply invented one morning early in the nineteenth century by a man looking at a map' (p. 9). Towards the end of his enormous narrative Farrell draws back from his panoramic vista of a war-torn city and adjusts the perspective, identifying Singapore as 'nothing but a tiny smudge on the horizon, insignificant' (p. 522). At the end of the book Farrell teasingly absconds from his narrative, leaving his characters with their destinies unresolved and reminding his readers of the fictionality of the novel which they have been reading:

there is a glimpse of garden in which a cat is trying to catch butterflies. . . . Or rather, no. Let us suppose that it is winter. Rub out the cat, erase the butterflies and let us move back inside where it is warmer. . . . it is suddenly summer again and a cat is trying to catch a butterfly. (pp. 566, 568)

The arbitrary, fantastic realm of Farrell's fictional terrain again seems to parallel *Alice's Adventures in Wonderland* and *Through the Looking Glass*. (Kate Blackett even resembles Alice, both in her baffled reactions to *Waterloo Bridge* and in her safe delivery from Wonderland – 'Singapore seems very far away now, and no longer quite real . . . a magical place where she spent her childhood' (p. 567).) General Percival finds himself in the situation of the Red King who (if Tweedledum and Tweedledee are to be believed) is dreaming everyone in Wonderland, and only with great difficulty restrains himself from fingering the Governor of Singapore, who he is convinced like 'Churchill, Wavell, Gordon Bennett, even his own staff, had no real substance . . . they were merely phantasms' (p. 553).

Although a novel full of fantastic comedy and parody *The Singapore Grip* also seeks to convey a serious analysis of colonialism, both locally, as it developed in Singapore, and in the global context of twentieth-century history. Farrell's novel looks back in time to the Boxer uprising of 1900, the Russian-Japanese war of 1905, the 1914–18 war, the South Manchuria crisis, Guernica and the developing unrest in French Indo-China (later Vietnam). The primary focus, however, is on the story of Blackett and Webb. Farrell begins by describing the preparations for a great carnival parade at the New Year of 1942 in order to celebrate the fiftieth anniversary of the founding of the firm in 1892:

It was felt that nothing could better demonstrate the benefits of British rule than to recall fifty years of one of Singapore's great merchant houses and the vast increase of wealth which it had helped to generate in the community for the benefit of all. (p. 34)

This provides the conventional conservative apologia for imperialism – an argument which Farrell proceeds to unravel in enormous detail as he examines, in a series of flashbacks and political dialogues, the development of Blackett and Webb from a small firm trading in tropical produce into a massive rubber concern. From its earliest days of dealing in opium and coolies Blackett and Webb is shown to be a ruthless, morally corrupt business devoted exclusively to the pursuit of greater and greater profit. Farrell follows the expansion of the firm from its seizure of control of the rice mills in 1893, its pre-1914 acquiring of plantations, and its increasing stake in the rubber market, through to the 1930s and the deliberate creation of an artificial rubber shortage. The narrative explores the vocabulary and practices of capitalism, investigating the role played in business life by equity, bond-holdings, commodity brokers, stocks and standard profit. Farrell's real intention is to amplify in considerable detail the conclusions reached by P. T. Bauer in his highly critical and unwelcome report on malpractices by the colonial administration in its treatment of native smallholders in the field of rubber growing. Bauer observed that rubber growing was highly suited to the Asian smallholder, since the technique of production and marketing was simple and did not depend on seasonal factors. He concluded that 'Rubber production is an industry where apart from statutory restriction, the small man was until recently in a position to start on his own and so secure a decent and independent income.'[57] But as Bauer showed, the native smallholders were being cynically restricted by statutory policies enforced by the Controller of Rubber to the benefit of the great estates.

Many reviewers found Farrell's detailed unveiling of the mechanics of colonial capitalism indigestible, but Timothy Mo praised the politics of the novel:

The account of the development of the big Far Eastern commercial houses, the rubber business, the way native small-holders were systematically ruined, the unholy alliance of Indian money-lenders and Western capital which

destroyed the old communities and created a pool of planta-
tion and mining labour, the rise of Japanese imperialism – all
this could be the work of a professional left-wing academic.
Maybe it is. Farrell lists 50 reference books.[58]

Certainly Farrell seems to have wanted *The Singapore Grip*
to be seen as a political novel,[59] but identifying the political
position which lies behind his economic critique of imperialism
is not easy. Farrell apparently read Marx and Engels while
writing *The Singapore Grip* and much of what passes through
Matthew Webb's mind might be identified as conventionally
Marxist in its thrust. But Matthew is unsympathetic to the idea
of revolution, and seems at heart to be a liberal. In the
bibliography attached to the novel Farrell pointedly does not
list the two best-known Marxist studies of imperialism (Rosa
Luxemburg's *The Accumulation of Capital* (1913) and
Lenin's *Imperialism* (1916)) but rather J. A. Hobson's influential and pioneering analysis *Imperialism* (1902). Hobson developed a liberal critique of imperialism as capitalism led
astray by self-interest (a contradiction in terms from a Marxist
point of view). Hobson identified export of capital as the major
cause of imperialism and attributed it to lack of investment
opportunity at home. His recommended solution was to raise
wages, thereby improving the purchasing power and living
standards of the population.

It seems unlikely that Farrell was wholeheartedly drawn to
Marxist analyses of imperialism since such studies often claim
to be scientific, and *The Singapore Grip* satirizes the idea of
scientific explanations of human behaviour. Sinclair asserts
that Asiatics 'are always killing each other. *It seems they don't
mind*. It's been proved scientifically' (p. 31), and Brooke-
Popham explains that the reason the Japanese are 'touchy and
arrogant' is because they eat too much fish: 'It's scientific. The
iodine in their diet plays hell with their thyroids' (p. 140).
Ehrendorf's First and Second Laws are perhaps intended as a
parody of Marx's 'natural laws' of capitalist production and
accumulation. A Marxist voice is heard in *The Singapore Grip*

in the form of the ragged British Tommy who harangues a drunken crowd with a speech attacking 'greedy profiteers in London' and the 'dirty capitalist war!' (pp. 558–9). But the man is a marginal figure and Farrell treats him unsympathetically, describing his speech as 'ranting' and comparing him to 'a wild animal' (p. 559). Matthew does on occasion, however, come out with some very radical propositions which are not subjected to irony. He angrily tells Ehrendorf:

> It's no good calling somebody free unless he's economically free, too, at least to some extent. . . . Is it? . . . however much lack of freedom may horrify an English intellectual sitting at his desk with a hot dinner under his belt. (p. 439)

In fact food, civilization and economics are closely intertwined in *The Singapore Grip*. Capitalism is represented as a nightmare world of ravenous profit-seeking: 'seething, devouring, copulating, businesses rose and fell, sank their teeth into each other, swallowed, broke away, gulped down other firms' (p. 12). Bestial images of sucking, swallowing and devouring run through the novel to evoke the workings of capitalism, and are paralleled by the lavish meals and parties at which Farrell's European characters gorge themselves on exquisite delicacies. At the end of the novel Farrell ironically juxtaposes two scenes, set wide apart in time but both to do with food and civilization. In one, Kate Blackett, the rubber tycoon's daughter, sits comfortably in her quiet Bayswater home eating her breakfast. In the other, Matthew Webb, the rubber tycoon's son, inhabits a Japanese prison camp: 'Accustomed to speculate grandly about the state and fate of nations he now found that his thoughts were limited to the smallest of matters . . . a glass of water, a pencil, a handful of rice' (p. 565).

Matthew, as the severest critic of the policies of Blackett and Webb, uses familiarly Farrellesque medical metaphors to convey the workings of his father's business. Profit, he remarks, took a *grip* on the country 'like some dreadful new virus against which nobody had any resistance' (p. 172), adding that 'the coming of Capitalism has really been like the spreading of a disease' (p. 174). The metaphor of the grip or stranglehold of capitalism is developed in a variety of ways through the novel. At first Matthew is merely puzzled by the mysterious, ribald warning to 'watch out for the Singapore Grip!' (p. 101) and he becomes involved in a protracted sequence of comic misunderstandings about the real meaning of this expression. Dupigny explains that it refers to a local fever, Ehrendorf believes it to refer to a suitcase, and Joan insists that it means a sort of hairpin. Its literal meaning – a sex technique of the Singapore whores – shades into a variety of other meanings in which prostitution and 'the grip of tuberculosis and malaria' (p. 217) are equally by-products of 'the grip of our Western culture and economy on the Far East' (p. 498). Colonial Singapore is an inherently parasitical society, something which is ironically underscored by Matthews's original impression from the air of

a number of miniature buildings scarcely big enough to house a colony of fleas . . . an open green space on which a fleas' cricket match was taking place . . . a cathedral . . . with one or two flea-worshippers scurrying . . . to offer up their evening prayers. (p. 101)

Perhaps the most effective way Farrell dramatizes his underlying message about colonial exploitation is through Walter Blackett's ambitious plans for a carnival parade celebrating his firm's jubilee. Walter, whose sense of irony is not strong, conceives of a float which will show 'Singapore in her relationship with the other trading centres of the Far East, holding them in a friendly grip' (p. 250) – namely 'as a sort of beneficial octopus with its tentacles in a friendly way encircling the necks of Shanghai, Hong Kong, Bombay, Colombo, Rangoon, Saigon and Batavia' (p. 250). These plans quickly develop into scenes of sheer farce. At the dress rehearsal the Major is obliged to dress up in a scarlet costume with horns and tails, personifying 'Inflation'; Monty's costume consists of an old striped swimming-costume, a fanged mask and talons, personifying 'Crippling Overheads'. Most preposterous of all is 'a symbolical rubber tree' (p. 361) which, supposed to represent wealth pouring from a tree as liquid gold, simply squirts coloured water. As the Major observes, instead of representing the intended meaning the tree appears to be urinating – a ribald and all-too-apt symbol of Blackett and Webb's real attitude to the native population.

The parade never takes place. The Japanese invasion of Malaya intervenes and the floats are cannibalized for use by the auxiliary fire service. It is decided that 'Prosperity' had better go before the float representing the variously coloured arms of the native population emerging from the jaws of 'Poverty', otherwise, as Dupigny sardonically observes, 'it might almost look as if the dollar bills were chasing the representatives of the four races and that they, arms outstretched, were fleeing in terror' (p. 425). Ultimately the floats are smashed in the air-raids and our last glimpse of Walter's grandiose scheme is of 'an untidy mass of broken spars and tattered paper' (p. 483).

Thomas Mann once identified *The Magic Mountain* as 'a dialectic novel'[60] and the same description might be applied to *The Singapore Grip*, which similarly diagnoses a corrupt community on the brink of apocalypse and military defeat. What Farrell presents is a variety of opinions and attitudes to Empire, ranging from Matthew Webb's liberal humanist critique to Walter Blackett's unquestioning acceptance of the status quo. Between these two sharply polarized viewpoints a number of other attitudes are represented, particularly those of Ehrendorf and Dupigny. Ehrendorf is a liberal-minded conservative. He disagrees with Matthew's critique of colonial economics, re-stating in conventional terms 'the benefits of western civilis-ation, the social welfare, education, medicine and so forth' (p. 175). Ehrendorf is at heart a pessimist and his experiences in Singapore finally lead him to the ironic discovery of 'Ehren-dorf's Second Law' – namely, that 'The human situation, in general or in particular, is slightly worse . . . at any given moment than at any preceding moment' (p. 284). Dupigny, a penniless refugee in his fifties, is even more despairing and cynical about human affairs than Ehrendorf. Dupigny (whose name may involve a pun on the French word *dupeur*, meaning 'trickster') is a total pessimist who holds deterministic Social Darwinian views about the way nations behave. Farrell ironically highlights the inadequacy of each of these characters. Dupigny, the cynical disbeliever in fraternity, finally relies on the selfless assistance of others when he injures his leg and is led away on a stretcher to a Japanese prison camp. The validity of Ehrendorf's Second Law is called into question by the manifest failure of his First Law, 'the survival of the easiest', according to which coffee beans, piano playing and the reading of books will all disappear in the near future. Finally, Matthew, who is literally short-sighted, is greatly discomforted in the Chinese dying-house by native criticisms of his father's business: 'he did not mind being critical of the British himself, but when a foreigner was critical, that was different' (p. 344).

At the heart of *The Singapore Grip* lies a comic vision of human muddle and confusion which develops into the partly-tragic, partly-farcical climax. The misinterpretation of signs and the misperception of each others' motives and behaviour which dogs Farrell's characters gives way to the darkness and confusion of the military battle for Singapore which, on the allied side, is significantly characterized by *communications difficulties*.

\*

What kind of lesson Farrell intends us to learn from *The Singapore Grip* and the two previous novels in his Empire trilogy is debatable. In the case of *The Singapore Grip* there is an obvious moral that the city's downfall was a deserved retribution for decades of colonial greed, privilege and exploitation. Margaret Drabble has asserted that Farrell's ironic narrative mode 'is directed towards one end – the revelation of the absurdity and injustice of things as they are, and the need for radical change', while adding the important proviso, 'How much faith he had in the possibility of change is another question' (*HS*, pp. 190–1).

The last, retrospective chapter of *The Singapore Grip*, where we might well expect the novelist to sum things up for us as

100

Tolstoy does in *War and Peace*, is profoundly ambiguous. It presents us with a mysterious grey-haired figure who may conceivably be Ehrendorf but who sounds suspiciously like the author himself, laconically intimating that despite imperial decay and wars the poor and exploited are still present on the earth in abundance and that nothing very much has changed in the world. As Walter Blackett remarks, quoting the chilling dictum of Lever of Lever Brothers, 'War is only a passing phase in business life' (p. 539).

Farrell's languid sense of irony and grim absurdist humour seem ultimately most to resemble the nonchalant, detached fireman Adamson (the son of Adam, perhaps), who 'managed to convey the impression that he was merely out for a stroll among the burning buildings' (p. 477). Adamson, more than anyone else, sees to the tragic core of the human condition:

> Adamson, leaning on his stick, was contemplating a battered old hairbrush with bristles splayed by use, a sponge-bag, a couple of books including a child's picture book, what might have been a cotton dress or apron and several other indeterminate pieces of cloth or clothing. He continued to gaze at these things for a moment with raised eyebrows and a grim expression on his face. . . . Matthew would remember for a long time to come that bitter, ironic expression he had glimpsed on Adamson's face as he limped away down the empty street after the dog which had already disappeared into the rolling smoke. (pp. 477–8)

In *The Lung* and *A Girl in the Head* Farrell's melancholy view of human life is conveyed with abrasive anger and a cold despairing wit. *Troubles* proposes a stoic resignation in the face of death and time. *The Siege of Krishnapur* ends in bitterness and weary, disgusted quietism. *The Singapore Grip* casts a wry, retrospective look back at these previous books. Ehrendorf's Second Law seems ironically accurate in terms of the widening social disintegration charted in the trilogy as a whole, and it is no accident that among the buildings of Singapore is the Majestic hotel, presumably engulfed like everything else by the general destruction. Singapore becomes literally 'under siege' (*SG*, p. 515) but the heroics witnessed at Krishnapur are not repeated. Although General Percival hoped to hold out for three months the walls of 'Fortress Singapore' were breached in little more than twenty-four hours, and the city capitulated after just ten days. Farrell in fact parodies both *Troubles* and *The Siege of Krishnapur*: the wise doctors of these two novels are replaced in *The Singapore Grip* by the blundering, foolish comic figure of Dr Brownley. Dr Ryan's solemn assertions about the tragic insubstantiality of human beings are cruelly parodied: '"People are like bubbles, Brendan," declared Dupigny in a sombre and sententious manner. "They drift about for a little while and then they burst"' (p. 463). Dupigny adds, 'narrowing his eyes in a Cartesian manner. "We are made of ninety-nine per cent water, we are like cucumbers"' (Ibid.). Dupigny, in short, is a resurrection of Boris from *A Girl in the Head*, but his cynicism is placed by his ignominious exit from the novel on a stretcher borne by the Major and Matthew.

The contradictory positions which Farrell's previous novels arrive at are restated but not resolved in *The Singapore Grip*. When the narrator shrugs off the immense and painful burden of his tale ('there is really nothing more to be said' (p. 568)), it is a remark one immediately wants to challenge. In *The Singapore Grip*, as in the trilogy as a whole, Farrell explores moral values and concepts of history and imperialism about which there will always be a great deal to say.

# NOTES

1  J. G. Farrell, 'Aristocrat', *Listener*, 2 November 1972, p. 611.
2  Georg Lukács, *The Historical Novel*, trans. Hannah and Stanley Mitchell (Harmondsworth, 1969), p. 20.
3  Colin Cross, *The Fall of the British Empire* (London, 1970), p. 365.
4  John Carey, 'Loti: a Many-splendoured Thing', *Sunday Times*, 23 October 1983.
5  David Holloway, 'Man for the Future', unidentified press cutting, Trinity College Farrell Collection, 9160.
6  Bernard Share, 'Respiratory Tract', unidentified press cutting, Trinity College Farrell Collection, 9160.
7  Elizabeth Bowen, 'Ireland Agonistes', *Europa*, 1, 1971, p. 59.
8  Ibid.
9  Lukács, op. cit., p. 78.
10 Bridget O'Toole, 'Books', *Fortnight*, 4 December 1970, p. 23.
11 Bowen, op. cit., p. 59.
12 A. N. Wilson, 'An Unfinished Life', *Spectator*, 25 April 1981, pp. 20–1.
13 Frank Kermode, *The Sense of an Ending* (London, 1968), p. 29.
14 Alasdair MacIntyre, 'The Strange Death of Social Democratic England', in David Widgery (ed.), *The Left in Britain 1956–68* (Harmondsworth, 1976), p. 235.
15 J. G. Farrell, 'No Matter', *Spectator*, 29 August 1970, p. 217.
16 Donald Horne, *The Great Museum* (London, 1984), pp. 121–2.
17 'J. G. Farrell Comments', in James Vinson (ed.), *Contemporary Novelists* (London, 1972), p. 399.
18 John Spurling, 'Jim Farrell', *The Times*, 11 April 1981, p. 6.
19 Margaret Drabble, 'Books of the Year', *Observer*, 17 December 1978, p. 33.

20  Timothy Mo, 'Magpie Man', *New Statesman*, 15 September 1978, p. 337.

21  Derek Mahon, 'J. G. Farrell', *New Statesman*, 31 August 1979, p. 313.

22  Unpublished letter to the author, 8 November 1978.

23  Mahon, op. cit., p. 313.

24  Charles Palliser, 'J. G. Farrell and the Wisdom of Comedy', *The Literary Review*, 5–18 October 1979, p. 14.

25  Paul Theroux, 'An Interrupted Journey', *Sunday Times*, 26 April 1981, p. 42.

26  John Osborne, 'Hooked on the Hill', *New Standard*, 28 April 1981.

27  A. N. Wilson, op. cit., p. 20.

28  Nicholas Shrimpton, 'Talent for Thought', *New Statesman*, 24 April 1981, p. 19.

29  V. G. Kiernan, *Marxism and Imperialism* (London, 1974), p. 80.

30  Victoria Glendinning, 'Farrell's Last Words', *Listener*, 23 April 1981.

31  Vladimir Nabokov, *Lolita* (London, 1961), p. 196.

32  E. Œ. Somerville and Martin Ross, *The Irish R.M.* (London, 1970), p. 508.

33  A. J. P. Taylor, *English History 1914–1945* (Harmondsworth, 1975), p. 206.

34  Ibid.

35  Susan Sontag, *Illness as Metaphor* (Harmondsworth, 1983), p. 14.

36  Ibid., pp. 18–19.

37  Patrick Skene Catling, 'Majestic Decay', *Spectator*, 21 May 1983, p. 29.

38  Edgar Allan Poe, 'The Fall of the House of Usher', in *Selected Writings* (Harmondsworth, 1967), p. 152.

39  Ibid., p. 139.

40  E. M. Forster, *A Passage to India* (Harmondsworth, 1961), p. 166.

41  Albert Camus, *Collected Fiction*, trans. Stuart Gilbert (London, 1960), p. 172.

42  Stendhal, *The Charterhouse of Parma*, trans. Margaret Shaw (Harmondsworth, 1967), p. 59.

43  Ibid., p. 82.

44  See Maev Kennedy, 'Farrell's Unfinished', *Irish Times*, 16 May 1981; Paul Theroux, op. cit.; John Spurling, 'As Does the Bishop' (*HS*, p. 164).

45  See William Empson, *Some Versions of Pastoral* (Harmondsworth, 1966).

46   Kiernan, op. cit., p. 84.
47   Thomas Mann, *The Magic Mountain*, trans. H. T. Lowe-Porter (Harmondsworth, 1960), p. 32.
48   Lucy Hughes-Hallett, 'War and Commerce', *Vogue*, 1 September 1978, p. 28.
49   Cross, op. cit., p. 240.
50   Ibid., p. 141.
51   Quoted in Frank Owen, *The Fall of Singapore* (London, 1962), p. 40.
52   John Mellors, 'Five Good Novels', *Listener*, 28 September 1978, p. 410.
53   *Book of the Month Club Magazine*, 40, n.d., p. 8.
54   L. N. Tolstoy, *War and Peace*, trans. Rosemary Edmonds, vol. I (Harmondsworth, 1961), p. 3.
55   Max Hastings, 'The Grip of Empire', *Evening Standard*, 10 October 1978, p. 22.
56   Isabel Quigly, 'Soldiering on in Singapore', *Financial Times*, 21 September 1978, p. 12.
57   P. T. Bauer, *Report on a Visit to the Rubber Growing Smallholdings of Malaya* (London, 1948), p. 87.
58   Mo, op. cit., p. 338.
59   When, prior to publication, I sent Farrell a copy of my review essay 'The Novelist as Historian' (*Critical Quarterly*, Summer 1979, pp. 70–2) in which I described *The Singapore Grip* as 'below the surface, a remarkably political novel' he wrote back 'I'm grateful that someone has read The S. G. [*sic*] as I hoped people would read it' (unpublished letter to the author, 8 November 1978).
60   Cited on the jacket of the Penguin edition (Harmondsworth, 1979).

# BIBLIOGRAPHY

## WORKS BY J. G. FARRELL

*Novels*

*A Man From Elsewhere*. London: Hutchinson, 1963.
*The Lung*. London: Hutchinson, 1965.
*A Girl in the Head*. London: Jonathan Cape, 1967. New York: Harper & Row, 1969.
*Troubles*. London: Jonathan Cape, 1970. New York: Knopf, 1971.
*The Siege of Krishnapur*. London: Weidenfeld & Nicolson, 1973. New York: Knopf, 1974.
*The Singapore Grip*. London: Weidenfeld & Nicolson, 1978. New York: Knopf, 1979.
*The Hill Station, an unfinished novel*. With Two Appreciations and a Personal Memoir, and an Indian Diary. London: Weidenfeld & Nicolson, 1981.

*Short fiction*

'The Pussycat Who Fell in Love with the Suitcase'. *Atlantis*, 6 (Winter 1973/4), pp. 6–10.

*Selected non-fiction*

'Tit bits'. *Spectator*, 17 January 1970, p. 84.
'Bonny and Clyde'. *Spectator*, 31 January 1970, p. 84.
'Miller's Tale'. *Spectator*, 7 March 1970, p. 310.
'Under the Seat'. *Spectator*, 6 June 1970, pp. 748–9.
'Old Wives' Tale'. *Spectator*, 20 June 1970, p. 822.
'The Army Game'. *Spectator*, 18 July 1970, p. 44.

'Hair Brained'. *Spectator*, 8 August 1970, p. 133.
'No Matter'. *Spectator*, 29 August 1970, p. 217.
'Girls and Boys'. *Spectator*, 10 October 1970, p. 407.
'Fat and Bloody'. *Listener*, 15 June 1972, p. 797.
'Brautigan Briefs'. *Listener*, 13 July 1972, p. 57.
'Sinking Feelings'. *Listener*, 7 September 1972, p. 312.
'Strindberg's Women'. *Listener*, 5 October 1972, pp. 447–8.
'Aristocrat'. *Listener*, 2 November 1972.
'J. G. Farrell Comments'. *Contemporary Novelists* (ed. James Vinson). London: St James Press, 1972, pp. 399–400.
'Late Lowry'. *New Statesman*, 19 July 1974, pp. 87–8.
'J. G. Farrell'. *Bookmarks* (ed. Frederick Raphael). London: Quartet, 1975, pp. 49–52.
'Complicated Tales'. *Guardian*, 5 October 1978, p. 14.
'All about India'. *Guardian*, 30 November 1978, p. 16.

### Papers

A collection of manuscripts, notebooks and press cuttings is held in the Library of Trinity College, Dublin. See *Papers of James Gordon Farrell (1935–1979)*, T.C.D. MSS 9128–60.

## SELECTED CRITICISM OF J. G. FARRELL

### Articles

Bergonzi, Bernard. 'Fictions of History'. In Malcolm Bradbury and David Palmer (eds), *The Contemporary English Novel*, pp. 42–65. London: Edward Arnold, 1979.
Binns, Ronald. 'The Novelist as Historian'. *Critical Quarterly*, 21, 2 (Summer 1979), pp. 70–2.
——'The Fiction of J. G. Farrell'. *Malcolm Lowry Newsletter*, 5 (Fall 1979), pp. 22–4.
Drabble, Margaret. 'Things Fall Apart'. Appended to J. G. Farrell, *The Hill Station, an unfinished novel*, pp. 161–72. London: Weidenfeld & Nicolson, 1981.
O'Toole, Bridget, 'J. G. Farrell'. In James Vinson (ed.), *Contemporary Novelists*, pp. 400–1. London: St James Press, 1972.
Palliser, Charles. 'J. G. Farrell and the Wisdom of Comedy'. *Literary Review*, 1 (5–18 October 1979), p. 14.
Spurling, John. 'As Does the Bishop'. Appended to J. G. Farrell, *The Hill Station, an unfinished novel*, pp. 141–60. London: Weidenfeld & Nicolson, 1981.

*Memoirs*

Dean, Malcolm. 'A Personal Memoir'. Appended to J. G. Farrell, *The Hill Station, an unfinished novel*, pp. 173–84. London: Weidenfeld & Nicolson, 1981.

Drabble, Margaret. 'Legacy of a Great Friendship'. *Sunday Telegraph Magazine*, 4 September 1983, pp. 16–17. Reprinted in Susan Hill (ed.), *People*, pp. 43–8. London: Chatto & Windus/Hogarth Press, 1983.

King, Francis. 'The Loner who loved Company'. *Sunday Telegraph*, 19 August 1979, p. 14.

Mahon, Derek. 'J. G. Farrell 1935–1979'. *New Statesman*, 31 August 1979, p. 313.

Spurling, John. 'J. G. Farrell'. *Observer*, 19 August 1979, p. 36.

——'Jim Farrell: a Memoir'. *The Times*, 11 April 1981, p. 6.

*Reviews*

Ackroyd, Peter. 'Insubstantial Pageant'. *Spectator*, 1 September 1973, pp. 282–3.

Anon. 'Down to the Bone'. *The Times Literary Supplement*, 21 September 1973, p. 1074.

Bowen, Elizabeth. 'Ireland Agonistes'. *Europa*, 1 (1970), pp. 58–9.

Brooks, Jeremy. 'Historical Novels: The yarn of Humanity'. *Sunday Times*, 17 September 1978, p. 41.

Catling, Patrick Skene. 'Majestic Decay'. *Spectator*, 21 May 1983, p. 29.

Enright, D. J. 'Tribal Lays'. *London Review of Books*, 7–20 May 1981, p. 6.

Hinde, Thomas. 'Passages to India'. *Sunday Telegraph*, 26 April 1981, p. 12.

King, Francis. 'Ritual of a Deathbed'. *Sunday Telegraph*, 16 September 1973, p. 12.

Lewis, Jeremy. 'Autumn Fiction'. *The Times*, 13 September 1978, p. 14.

Mahon, Derek. 'Halfway up the Magic Mountain'. *Observer*, 26 April 1981, p. 32.

Mo, Timothy. 'Magpie Man'. *New Statesman*, 15 September 1978, pp. 337–8.

O'Toole, Bridget. 'Books'. *Fortnight*, 4 December 1970, p. 23.

——'A Bizarre, Coherent World'. *Honest Ulsterman* (June–October 1981), pp. 59–60.

Porterfield, Christopher. 'Deluded Idyll'. *Time*, 29 May 1979, pp. 69, 72.

Shrimpton, Nicholas. 'Talent for Thought'. *New Statesman*, 24 April 1981, p. 19.

Simpson, David. 'After the Siege'. *British Medical Journal*, 18 April 1981, pp. 1287–8.

Symons, Julian. 'Heading for a Fall'. *The Times Literary Supplement*, 6 October 1978, p. 1110.

Theroux, Paul. 'An Interrupted Journey'. *Sunday Times*, 26 April 1981, p. 42.

Thwaite, Anthony. 'Chopping through History'. *Observer*, 17 September 1978, p. 34.

Webb, W. L. 'New Books'. *Guardian*, 29 November 1973, p. 10.

Wilson, A. N. 'An Unfinished Life'. *Spectator*, 25 April 1981, pp. 20–1.